QUINCY'S
WAR

Herbert Angstrom

QUINCY'S
WAR

THE STORY *of*
JOHN QUINCY ADAMS
CIVIL WAR BUGLER

35th
MASSACHUSETTES
VOLUNTEER
INFANTRY

By His Great Grandson
ANDREW HERBERT ANGSTROM

NORTHLOOP
BOOKS

NORTH LOOP BOOKS

2301 Lucien Way #415
Maitland, FL 32751
407.339.4217
www.NorthLoopBooks.com

ISBN-13: 978-1-54560-108-2

Distributed by Itasca Books

Cover Design by: James Arneson
Typeset by: James Arneson

Printed in the United States of America

CONTENTS

Artistic license captures the furry of the charge over Burnside Bridge at Antietam Creek. Courtesy of the Library of Congress

FOREWORD

I have read a number of books on the U.S. Civil War, all of which included very stirring, and sometimes firsthand, accounts of the action. Many had historic pictures often taken soon after a battle. But the most fascinating aspect for me was the individual accounts by the participants, told in their own words, some elegant, some rough, in letters and diaries written during their service in the field. Unlike the historical records, these personal histories served to erase the time between the soldiers' experiences and my reading of them. They became people I might have met and spoken with at a gathering last week, rather than an almost fictional "anyone" from the distant past.

Another dimension of this "time-travel" encounter occurred to me the first time I visited a Civil War battle site. My daughter was researching material for a college paper on war memorials. I had often heard my brother speak of trips to Gettysburg National Military Park. Being about a 4.5-hour ride from my home in Ulster County, New York, we decided to drive there one morning, spend half a day there, stay locally, and come home the next morning. The area has been well preserved and, from any number of places at the site, one can well imagine it is a different century. Its effect on us was quite dramatic, and as experience-sharing as the personal records. We ended up spending a second entire day at the park and driving home late at night.

There is a time in the life of all things between when their usefulness ends or they become "outdated," and when they have achieved enough antiquity to be valued as symbols of an earlier, somewhat well-defined "era." It is a precarious time in the item's life. Many never survive long enough to acquire this antique value and are lost and often lamented by a later generation. Many Civil War sites can be found in both the saved and lost categories. The same can be said of family histories. It is the rare youngster who takes an interest in the stories of older generations. Not a few end up in adulthood searching fruitlessly for some relative who might recall lost knowledge that some years earlier would have been easily passed to the next generation.

This book is about a quest that was, happily, not unproductive. But it is more than simply a recounting of a successful history search. It is designed to inform those who may be contemplating a similar quest into the past. It may involve ancestors or not. Houses and neighborhoods have pasts as well, rooted in the activities of those who lived there.

My brother, a retired educator, found many helpful aids in this family search and presents them here with the purpose of encouraging others to pursue their own quest. Not the least helpful resource has been other family members who found their own interest in the pursuit grow as they saw the project take shape and their input affect the result.

In a letter we discovered written to my mother by my great-grandfather who fought in the war, he expresses his desire to revisit Antietam on the anniversary of that battle, because "there are always some Union and Confederate veterans there at that time" with whom he obviously enjoyed meeting. I imagine them walking over the former battlefields sharing stories about their experiences, widening their vision, their understanding, of the events they lived through. Men who were once shooting at each other, now joined by the common experience of survival

At peace now, the serenity of the Lower Bridge over Antietam Creek at Sharpsburg, Maryland, belies the maelstrom which took place on September 17, 1862, "The Bloodiest Day." General Burnside had ordered the Thirty-Fifth Massachusetts and the three other regiments of General Ferrero's Brigade, the Ninth Corps, to charge across under heavy fire for the hill above.

and the desire for the revelations of an authentic alternative viewpoint to the battles in which they fought.

We hope this book will not only present the story of a young soldier and his great adventure, but also the process by which that story unfolded, and thus encourage you to pursue history, entering into the adventure of encountering people, places, and events of your own past.

By Michael Louis Angstrom,

Quincy's Great-Grandson

The old house in Alpine, New York, as we knew it.

INTRODUCTION

Quincy's War isn't about blood and gore, or glory, it's the story of a young man caught up in the adventure of a lifetime, and a grand, horrific, and defining time for a young nation. Quincy wasn't a new immigrant from the bowels of Boston or a hardened farm lad; nor was he the son of a family of born warriors. He was from a good, old New England family, and music was his passion. Quincy was well educated for his time and age, so he was able to record his experiences in the form of letters and even a diary and later share them with the folks back home. The family's care in preserving his artifacts for future generations made it possible for me to attempt this reconstruction of "Quincy's war."

I have many wonderful childhood memories of Grandma and Grandpa Adams' home. The 1830s farmhouse in rural Alpine, New York, was a wonder in itself; it still had a wood-boxed, hand-crank telephone in the late 1940s when I first remember visiting my maternal grandparents! I remember one time when "Gramma" "rang up" the little general store down at the crossroads: two longs and a short was the store's code. The phones in all the other houses in Alpine would ring, but only the store was supposed to answer that code. The call was powered by the dry cell batteries in Grandma's phone, so with each new busybody listening in, the responding store clerk's voice would weaken. Grandma would scold, "Oh for Pete's sake, will some of you hang up so I can hear!" I also remember playing in the huge barn, exploring the treasure trove that was the attic, and listening to ghost stories in the parlor . . . and that wonderful old bugle! Try as I might, I was never able to blast out more than one note on that magnificent thing. We kids were reverently reminded many times by Grandma that it was the Civil War bugle of John Quincy Adams, Grandpa's father. I remember always being confused by that; wasn't he also a president or something?

His hat was another "sacred relic" that we were always shown but could never touch; after all, there were thirteen of us little cousins, all wannabe soldiers.

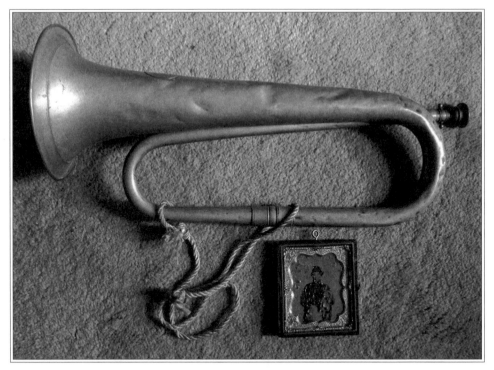

Quincy's bugle and photo, which both hung on Grandma's wall

I am now the keeper of the hat, entrusted to me by my aunt, the youngest and last of Quincy's four granddaughters. Realizing the value of these heirlooms in the telling of his story, I contacted the grown members of the ever-multiplying and diversifying clan, and suggested a plan to record and preserve them before it was too late. I have made it my quest to begin this process and tell his story. If this work serves no other purpose, it will be worthwhile. However, I hope that it also serves as an inspiration and even a model or template for my readers to repeat the process for their own family heroes, warriors or not.

Many tens of thousands of young men, who would have had amazing and exciting stories, never survived their ordeals: killed in action or dead from ghastly wounds after the army moved on . . . or from poor medical practices or disease, which almost precluded Quincy's story. I am sure many more were too sick of fighting and killing and wanted nothing more than to forget. Still more were illiterate and couldn't have expressed their experiences in writing. And how many war diaries were lost, or ruined, as Quincy's might have been, from the years 1862 and 1864? How many were simply thrown away in later years by disinterested or neglectful family members? This undertaking will collect, preserve, and share that which Quincy and his family so dutifully bequeathed.

His hat! Pictured here is not the kepi or forage cap he is shown to be wearing in at least one photo and most certainly wore during his war. It is, of course, his Grand Army of the Republic (G.A.R.) hat. The G.A.R. was the most widespread of the Union veterans' groups. His post number is displayed in the wreath. Not being a military hat expert, it appears to me to be a crumpled model 1858 "Hardee" hat with a slough hat's posture: the first a very formal-looking cover; the other a more casual, comfortable, and maintenance-free piece of essential clothing. And yes! He did survive the war and lived a long and fruitful life.

Great-Grandpa's "army hat"

DISCOVERING QUINCY: OKAY, SO HE WASN'T THE PRESIDENT! WHO WAS QUINCY?

February 17, 1844: John Quincy Adams is born to George Whitefield Adams and Louisa Morrill (Tandy) Adams of Manchester, New Hampshire.

George Whitefield Adams, 1815–1881: George Whitefield, John's father, was from New Hampshire. The Adams's were among the first Europeans to settle in America. Adam, arguably the oldest of male names in Christendom, was to become a very common surname in the British Isles, taking many forms. Following the patriarchal lineage of the New England Adams's back six generations from Quincy, you will come to Robert Adams, who as best as we can tell, came with his brother, William, to Massachusetts in 1635. William was the progenitor of the Adams branch that led to John Adams, second president of these United States, and his, son John Quincy, Adams, the sixth president and a lawyer for the defense in the famous Amistad case. In England, brothers Robert and William can be traced in a direct line back sixteen generations to Sir John Ap Adam, Baron and Knight of the Realm in the court of King Edward I. Sir John is said to have come out of the Marches of Wales. He bore the arms, pictured here, at the Battle of Falkirk, in Scotland in 1298. This battle was one of the few major actions won by the English in the first Scottish war for independence.

Louisa Morrill (Tandy) Adams, 18??–1873: Louisa was the daughter of Eliza (Morrill) Tandy, whose people lived in Maine and New Hampshire. Her

Most Massachusetts regimental flags displayed on both sides the Commonwealth's coat of arms, centered on a white field. The shield depicts an Algonquin Native American man with bow and arrow; the arrow is pointed downward, signifying peace. A white star with five points appears next to the figure's head, signifying Massachusetts' admission as the sixth U.S. state. A blue ribbon (blue signifying the Blue Hills of Canton and Milton) surrounds the shield, bearing the state motto, *"Ense Petit Placidam, Sub Libertate Quietem"* ("By the sword we seek peace, but peace only under liberty"). Above the shield is the state military crest: a bent arm holding a broadsword aloft. The sword has its blade up, to remind us that it was through the American Revolution that independence was won. The state flag was made official in 1908, but had been used unofficially since the American Revolution. This flag included on its reverse the blue shield from the coat of arms containing only a green pine tree, which had been the design of the state naval ensign ever since the Revolutionary War.[*] Courtesy of the Commonwealth of Massachusetts.

John ap Adam

---

[*]   Website of the Secretary of the Commonwealth of Massachusetts, "The History of the Arms and Great Seal of the Commonwealth of Massachusetts": http://www.sec.state.ma.us/pre/presea/sealhis.htm

father was Richard Tandy of the Pequot Nation, an Algonquin people. Interestingly, the Massachusetts coat of arms displays on its shield an Algonquin. These arms, or its crest, were emblazoned on many of the flags of the Commonwealth's volunteer infantry regiments.

Quincy's folks were about as New England as you could get. Quincy was a Yankee!

Okay, so Quincy wasn't the president. So who was he? "Quincy," as his family and friends, and presumably his comrades, called him, was born and grew up in Haverhill, Essex County, Massachusetts, a city of about ten thousand people in 1860. It was and is located about thirty miles due north of downtown Boston.

There is a family legend that tells of Quincy lying about his age to get into the army. Without his birth certificate, this is difficult to either substantiate or disprove. My research shows that boys as young as eight or ten frequently accompanied volunteer units into battle as bugle boys and drummers, and that there were relaxed age restrictions for musicians

An unlabeled albumen print from the Adams family archive, believed to be of Quincy in his youth, taken by Anderson Studio, 30 Merrimack Street, Haverhill, Massachusetts

in general. It is possible that Quincy may have tried to enlist as an infantryman by "exaggerating" his age at the time of Lincoln's public proclamation of April 1861, which called for "75,000 militia to still the insurrection". Existing evidence attests that he would have been seventeen at that time. Whatever the truth, Quincy's zeal to join the cause was above doubt and he volunteered when a local regiment was formed the following year.

)I(

I began the search to fill in the unknowns of Quincy's story with an Internet search of his military record. The Adams descendants were by this time very numerous and John was a very common name. When I typed his name into the search box of my Internet search engine, Walla! There were 438 Adams's in Civil War military units from Massachusetts alone; fifty-five of them were John Adams's and there were sixteen John Q. Adams's. I am guessing that all the "Q's" stood for Quincy.

There were a number of things we knew about Quincy because the family had preserved many of his artifacts and other memorabilia. Also, my mother and her three sisters had become interested in the family's genealogy and had done considerable work running down all sorts of family ties. I had already decided to gather all this and preserve and share it digitally with the ever-growing family before the material disappeared. One of the first items I photographed was an obviously old ink blotter, or so I thought, with a colorfully decorated front side. It turned out not to be a blotter but rather a Reward for Merit. I thought it was just a curio but eventually I discovered the very faded names of the recipient and the presenter. After enhancing the photo I had taken of it, I could read the name: John Q. Adams. It was most likely presented to him in grammar school, judging by the style and pictured subjects. This would make it from about the 1850s; parents today often save such memories of at least the first few kids.

A well-preserved "Reward of Merit," presented to John Q. Adams by Jane Downs, his instructor. The cherubs and classical figures suggest that it is a grammar school item. It was at first thought to be an ink blotter, common in schools where straight pen-and-ink sets were used. Digital enhancing brought out the almost invisible names.

Quincy was a musician. What his occupation was in 1862, we don't know, but after the war he would become a music teacher. Perhaps he could read and write better than most; he often wrote letters, and received them from home. He could probably read music at that time, too. In those days before telephones, e-mail, and social networking, letters were the everyday intra-family long-distance communication method. It was apparent from his journal that letters were exchanged often and were an important part of his military life. They were so frequent that it was customary to provide only the day of the week and A.M. or P.M. Rarely was the date or year included. Apparently, this was a custom of the time and was pervasive in Quincy's communications even after the war. Many of his surviving postwar letters would be dated simply "Monday Morning." This presented a big problem for the historical researcher attempting to reconstruct a timeline.

Quincy's journal of 1863 and a few letters were the primary sources for specific dates and places in his story. I scoured my own library of two dozen or so books on the Civil War as a refresher for the basics. These books, the educational TV channels, and many trips to battlefields had given me a fairly good understanding of the war. However, to recreate a more complete picture

of Quincy's war experience, I would need more specific sources. I decided I would use the story of his unit, the Thirty-Fifth Massachusetts Volunteer Infantry Regiment, as a starting place; this was, after all, his large, mobile, extended family. Company G became his more immediate family, its officers serving as surrogate parents. Unless a "family" member deserted, was on leave, or was too seriously wounded or sick to move on . . . or dead, he was with his unit. Since Quincy didn't desert and transportation logistics made an extended leave very unlikely, if not impossible, I have presumed him present and accounted for during the duration of his tour with the Thirty-Fifth. He did get sick, with at least one stop off at a hospital. Pneumonia eventually took him out of the war.

Quincy's closed journal

)I(

When I first received Quincy's diary, I quickly realized that I wouldn't be able to just read it like a modern book. There were several problems. The book was almost 150 years old and it had not been stored in a museum vault. Its first year of use had been the toughest; weather and camp life had beaten it up in its youth. It had been soaked badly at least once and the stains showed clearly as a "high-water mark" of penetration. The attached leather cover had been made fragile by time and handling; oxidation had yellowed it and light had both bleached the pages and faded the words. Varying grades of India ink and different pens, as well as graphite pencils, had been used. The penciled words were faint, but some of the inks were worse. Fortunately both graphite and India ink are carbon based and durable, unlike some of today's ink pigments. One type of ink, presumably obtained from a more reputable Sutler, was of higher carbon content, preserved better and therefore much easier to read one hundred and fifty years later. It took me awhile to recognize the differences. Unlike the ballpoint pens of today, the common straight and fountain pens of that time were made of a flat stock and had a wider tip like a calligraphy pen, producing a line wide to narrow then back again, depending on the angle.

When I went to grade school in the late 1940s and early '50s, my class was among the last to learn penmanship using the straight pen; fountain pens were the standard issue for grown-ups. We got to use these antiquated weapons, to the joy of all the boys, who played stick-the-pen-in-the-wooden-floor . . . while the teacher was working with the other thirty kids . . . and to the horror of the girls, who had to try to concentrate while the boys behind them schemed up yet other ways to maneuver their curls into the waiting inkwell. In order to actually use one of these primitive devices for writing, you would have to first dip the pen in the inkwell. Then you'd move the pen in place over the paper without depositing a blob of ink, push the now-jagged point across the paper in the shape of the desired letters until the ink line became too weak to read, and then repeat the process many times just to complete a paragraph. The successful completion of a sentence did not of itself guarantee proper penmanship, spelling, or syntax, of course. The relative lack of ink blobs in the journal probably indicates that Quincy used a fountain pen at least part of the time.

Quincy had his own interesting writing style, which took awhile to get used to. First I had to decipher the individual letters and words. They were almost always the lines of an exhausted young man quickly sprawling down a thought or two in the fading light of day or by candle. I myself had trouble managing this task at my wooden school desk, so I had a special appreciation for doing this in Quincy's circumstance. All things considered, his handwriting would have gotten me at least an A- in penmanship.

)I(

Quincy had a functioning family at home, including at least a caring, albeit austere looking father in George Whitefield Adams. A thoughtful letter from his dad survives and Quincy mentions letters from and to various others, including a girl named Mary, perhaps another relative or a lady friend. No letters from his brothers or his mother, Louisa, were found. Louisa would pass away in 1873, in her fifties. Quincy had three brothers: The Reverend Frank E., George M., and Charles H. Adams. All five names of his immediate family appear on the first page verso (left side) of his water-stained diary of 1863; they were, after all, his next of kin. Their names, along with his father and mother, were written in ink and are just discernible on the first page.

Quincy's next of kin, written on the first page of his 1863 journal. This view of the page has been digitally enhanced to bring out faded pen strokes. The "high-water mark" of soaking is clearly evident.

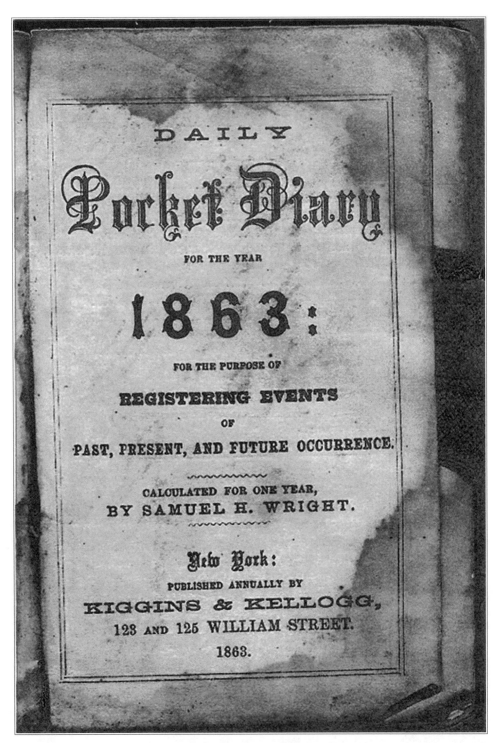

DAILY

Pocket Diary

FOR THE YEAR

1863:

FOR THE PURPOSE OF

REGISTERING EVENTS

OF

PAST, PRESENT, AND FUTURE OCCURRENCE.

CALCULATED FOR ONE YEAR,

BY SAMUEL H. WRIGHT.

New York:

PUBLISHED ANNUALLY BY

KIGGINS & KELLOGG,

123 AND 125 WILLIAM STREET.

1863.

Second page recto (right side) of John Quincy Adams's journal

DECIPHERING QUINCY'S JOURNAL

W*ebster's New World Dictionary* defines a "diary" and a "journal" to be exactly the same thing, except that in the definition of a journal, the word "happenings" takes the place of the diary's word "experiences." The difference seems to be the way events were recorded. When I read Quincy's diary, I was a little surprised. I guess I expected that a musician would write about how he feels about the rain, but he doesn't. He just says it's raining. I decided I was reading a journal.

Another of my cousins had accepted the guardianship of Quincy's journal several years ago and was in the process of carefully protecting it for our generation. When I approached him with the idea of sharing it digitally with all the family, he graciously agreed and turned it over to me to decipher and share. It appeared to be in relatively good condition. However, it was almost 150 years old and had obviously been water-soaked long ago, perhaps during the countless miles of rainstorms and stream crossings it had endured in a leaking canvas knapsack, or later in a leaky tent. Written in ink and at times pencil on thin pages of now-oxidizing paper, it was difficult to read. The space provided for each day was only 1¼ inches by 2½ inches. Quincy often filled that space with seven lines of text, a full page being able to hold only about two to three dozen words. The handling of these pages by many generations of relatives and their visitors as it was passed around the kerosene-lit parlors of the past, didn't help to enhance its fading words.

〉〉〈

When I first began to study the journal, I vowed to always wear a clean pair of those white cotton gloves you see museum guys using—when I remembered to, that is. I finally went to thin food-handling gloves as they were a lot cheaper and easier to come by. I began keeping several pairs of these gloves with the journal. I had also purchased a set of stackable plastic containers from a well-known super-chain store, to safely house all the artifacts, photographs, and documents related to this project while I was working on them and afterward. I keep the collection in low light at room temperature and low humidity, as sunlight and excess moisture will quickly age or destroy many items.

Rather than expose the delicate written items to further abuse, I carefully photographed or scanned each page of the journal and the letters into a digital .jpg file format. I then resealed the original items in plastic sleeves made for that purpose. After backing up the digital files on a separate storage device, I worked only with these digital copies on my PC from then on. This was the best and easiest way to complete the deciphering process. I could enlarge and enhance the files if necessary. I ended up with copies of the files that would be easier to read and to share with family members and eventually the public. At some point I decided "Why stop there?" given the ever-growing ranks of Civil War enthusiasts as well as folks who are interested in undertaking their own search for their heritage. So, I decided to write the story of Quincy's war.

The inside front cover and first page of Quincy's journal where he has written his name in two places and his brother Frank has added a presentation note. The book itself was apparently a gift and is inscribed: *Presented to John Q Adams by his brother Frank E. Adams, Haverhill Mass.* Notice the intensity of the two different inks. This photo has not been enhanced.

Some photographs and scans are in natural color, but I found it handy for deciphering purposes to auto-enhance most of the pages of my copied set to brighten the faded words. Not every six-day page pair had entries, so it wasn't necessary to enhance those. The digital format made it easy to magnify and further enhance areas that were excessively faded. I could also print out any page quickly, take it elsewhere to work on whenever I had a few minutes, or pass it to others to get their take. This process required no special equipment other than my laptop, a small flatbed scanner, and a standard home printer. This is all equipment most computer users have these days. I decided to include a few journal pages here for several reasons. They show different degrees of fading, mostly because Quincy used several different writing utensils. They also show different examples of penmanship. All are meant to provide the reader with the experience of deciphering Quincy's handwriting.

When I first opened the journal I found seven separate sheets numbered on the reverse 1 through 7. They were divided into ten sections, a line drawn between each. Each section began with a day and date starting with "Thursday, Feb. 5, 1863," and proceeding consecutively through "Tuesday, Feb. 17, 1863." These same days and dates had written entries in the journal. Upon checking, I realized that the words were essentially the same as those in the same dates of the journal itself. The seven separate sheets were written in pencil in a larger script and the paper was of a different type. Shown here is the third in the series. The graphite pencil lines have a more uniform thickness than those of the pencil and most of the inks used in the journal. As a result they were considerably easier to read than their equivalent entries in the journal.

Pencils in those days were usually made with sticks cut from natural graphite; the line formed is relatively durable but is gray rather than the dark black of

One of seven separate pages (not enhanced) found in Quincy's journal; it was written in pencil and well preserved.

India ink. The graphite stick could be mounted in a metal handle for strength and convenience in holding. The pencil was more convenient and did not require carrying extra ink in a bottle, which is subject to breaking, spilling, and freezing.

These seven pages puzzled me and presented a mystery that would require further consideration later.

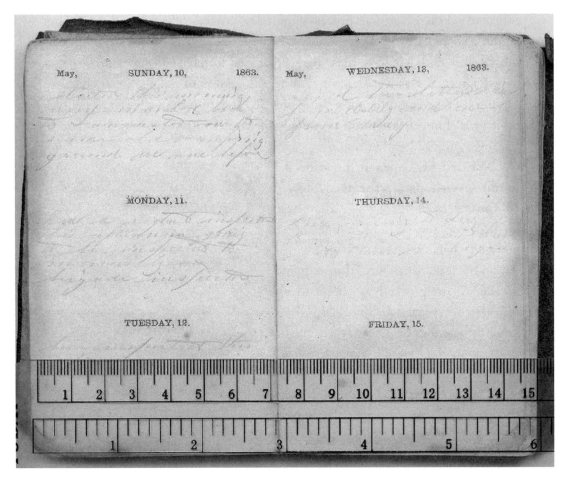

A sample open page of the journal written in an ink that had faded; there are entries on five days. The difficulty in reading the faded words is apparent in this true color photo.

When I finally started the deciphering process in earnest, I found that even when the letters were relatively clear I wasn't always sure what they were. Was that an "I" or a "j", an "n" or a "u"? Sometimes only certain pen or pencil strokes would be visible. Was that an "l" or an "h"? Differences in spelling or misspelling further complicated things. Was a "bout" the misspelling of the word "boat" (the context worked for "boat"), or was that the way it was spelled in those days? I have since noticed that "bout" was used in several other sources. There were of course a few obviously phonetically misspelled words, but generally his spelling wasn't bad for a youth in 1863. At the same age I wouldn't have wanted to compete in a spelling bee against Quincy. Viva la spell-check!

In order to make the deciphering process more fluent, I developed a letter specimen chart to record examples of Quincy's upper and lowercase letters and numbers. The first attempt by a relative to transcribe his "Bound for Memphis" letter had inadvertently transcribed the date as 1862. This is the only war-time letter of Quincy's in the family's collection and is presented in a later chapter. It was written during his steamboat transit down the Mississippi River. The 1862 date didn't make any sense from a geographical/historical perspective. Steamboats weren't time machines. Studying the original letter and comparing it with my chart clearly showed that the date was 1863. Now the date fit and made sense.

Using the two script styles closest to that of the journal, available on the Microsoft Word program in my PC, this chart was constructed. The first is Times New Roman, the second is *Brush Script*, and the third is *Edwardian Script*, all font size 19.

Sheet used to identify Quincy's letter formation for deciphering the text

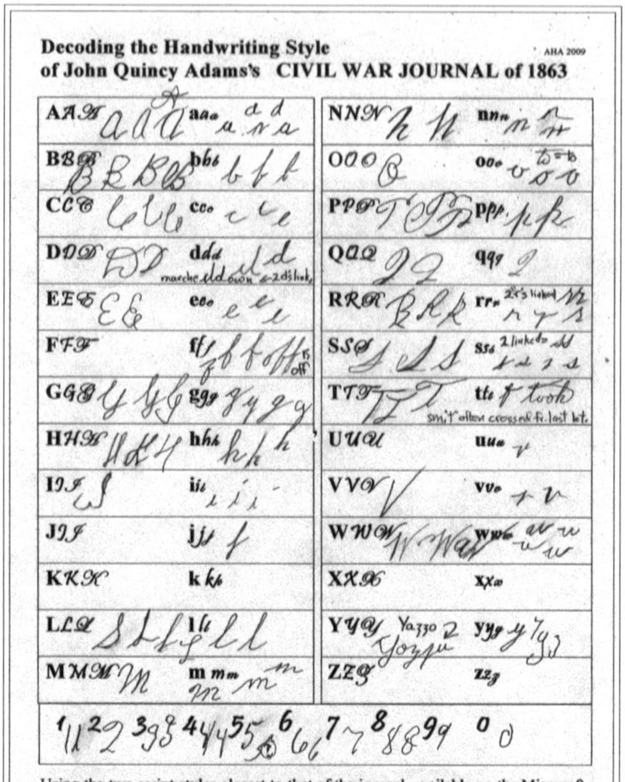

At times Quincy's pen and ink set were well matched, the pen producing a broad stroke and a durable ink that made the deciphering task easier. The enhanced page shown here is one of the easier ones to decipher. It also is a nice sample of action and poignancy. I have included it here to share with the reader the experience of Quincy's words, words that hadn't been read for almost 150 years.

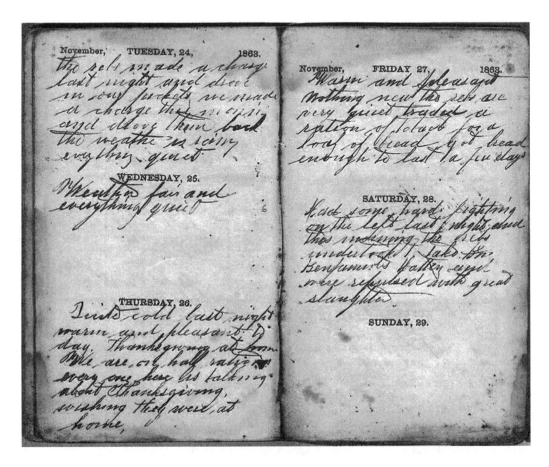

Pictured is a pair of the digitally enhanced pages of Quincy's journal. They were written in a more durable ink than many of the pages and provide the reader an opportunity to experience the deciphering process. The apparent yellowing of the old document paper varies with the enhancement process. The deciphering of this and all the other pages of Quincy's journal will follow in order.

EVALUATING QUINCY'S ARTIFACTS

Quincy's other memorabilia needed to be stabilized, catalogued, and digitally photographed or scanned. The collection, now spread out among a couple of cousins and Quincy's remaining granddaughter, was relatively easy to locate. The family has always stayed in touch, even holding occasional reunions. We all get along well, perhaps a legacy passed down by Quincy through his only child, my grandfather, Herbert Carroll Adams, and then to Herbert's four daughters, Virginia, Ellen (my mother), Alice, and Barbara.

Several different cousins all gladly offered up their Quincy holdings, for this process. These were: a bugle and hat, several tintypes, a small ambrotype, several larger albumen prints, a carte de visite or CDV, later reprints of old photographs of Quincy and related family members, a rectangular G.A.R. belt plate, newspaper clippings, a book of sheet music, two wartime letters, and seven postwar letters. The eldest and most elegant of my cousins told me about "Great-Grandpa's army stuff" she had: his mess kit, his army suit buttons, and more old pictures. As high on the "wonderful cousin scale" as she is, her interest in "old army stuff" wasn't at the level of a history nut such as me. However, she had been dutifully protecting these treasures since her folks had passed away, and when the opportunity came along, she seemed relieved to be able to pass them on to a responsible family member.

When I went to visit my cousin and the collection in her home in Washington Irving country, on the east banks of the majestic Hudson River in upstate New York, she had placed on the kitchen table what to my eyes was a veritable treasure trove of ancestral memorabilia. You can imagine my surprise when I saw immediately that there was a waist belt with a federal plate of 1851, and that it had a cartridge box attached to it. A shoulder and sword sling straps were missing; only a sword hanger hook was present. Sword sling straps were used to lower the sword attachment points when on horseback; apparently the soldier that wore this belt was not normally mounted. Only mounted troops, officers, and sergeants normally wore swords. Some musicians were also allowed swords but there is no evidence that Quincy carried a weapon. Was this stuff Quincy's?

Pictured above is the Civil War–era U.S. sword belt with hook, cartridge box and belt plate of 1851 from the Herbert Adams family collection. The shoulder strap and sword hanger straps are missing. This equipment was regulation issue for anyone in the Union Army authorized to carry a sword. Below are close-ups of the cartridge box and the sword hook for hanging the sword and scabbard.

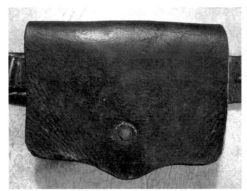

At this point I should tell you that for many years I have been a metal-detecting enthusiast. No, not a treasure hunter, but a "history hunter." I have concentrated on my part of the mid–Hudson Valley, the area around Kingston, New York. Kingston is in Ulster County and is the third-oldest non aboriginal settlement in New York State as well as the state's first Capital. It was settled by the Dutch in 1652 and torched two different times, once during the Esopus Wars by the native people in 1663, and once by the British under General John Vaughan in 1777. In the eyes of the British it was, after all, "a pestiferous nest of traitors".

In thirty years of hunting old farmsteads and any other places where I could get permission, I was lucky enough to be the first one to search several really old places and was able to amass a fairly respectful collection of local artifacts. I have been able to work many of them into my teaching in the Outdoor Education program at the Ashokan Field Campus of State University College at New Paltz, New York, now the Ashokan Center for Nature, Music and the Arts. Incidentally, this is the magical place that inspired Jay Ungar and Molly Mason to create *Ashokan Farwell,* which was then used by Ken Burns as the theme music for the PBS mini-series, *The Civil War.*

I have discovered and researched enough military equipages to become reasonably well versed in nineteenth-century uniform belt plates, buttons, and pins.

I refer to this as "history hunting" because each discovery I made would give me a personal connection to a piece of the past. Each of these connections became a doorway to further exploration and more discoveries. For instance, I first learned about one of our fascinating local militias by the finding of one old button. It turned out to be that of the Ulster Guard, or the old Twentieth New York. Many of the men folk in my area were veterans of this regiment and inevitably wore their old uniform jackets around the farm. This allowed me to eventually find not one but three of their unique buttons, on which was embossed ULSTER GUARD beneath the eagle-on-globe of New York State. An existing militia regiment, it became at first a "ninety-day unit," after which it was designated the Eightieth New York, but only on payday I am told. In the hearts and minds of its men it remained the Twentieth on all other days. I had to know more about this intriguing regiment. I discovered that the regiment fought at South Mountain, Antietam, and Fredericksburg, as did Quincy and the Thirty-Fifth Mass. At Gettysburg there now stand two monuments to the unit, emblazoned with an open right hand, its genesis likely from the symbol of Ulster, the northernmost province of Ireland.

Uniform coat button of the Ulster Guard, Twentieth New York State Militia (ca. 1850s), recovered in Ulster County, New York. The eagle-on-globe is from the New York State seal.

)I(

The very first military item I ever found was a magnificent early belt plate of a pattern that I still cannot find in any of the books, but is similar to those of the 1810s–20s. It came from the side yard to a small frame farmhouse that was all but gone. The second plate I found was one of the 1851 pattern. Both display renditions of the Great Seal. The rectangular plate of 1851 is very similar to the one discovered in the Adams collection. When I show these finds to folks, they often ask me how I found them up here, so far from the seat of war. The answer is simple. I believe that most old and obsolete, but still-functional items of clothing were worn for years afterward. Veterans often

U.S. sword belt plate, ca. 1810–20, recovered in Ulster County, New York. This is an early rendition of the national symbol used on a panoply of military items. The plate was probably for militia use. It is thought to be very rare.

wore their military coats in civilian life, as a badge of sorts or just working around the yard or farm, just as you might see a civilian today wearing an old army jacket. In those days clothes were often worn until they disintegrated. A very good friend of mine has found seven large George Washington inaugural buttons scattered around the yard of his federal-period farmhouse in Columbia County, New York. He says that a great coat of that period usually had eight buttons. He is still looking for the eighth one!

It is also very likely that when people and memories faded, once-treasured war trophies and souvenirs eventually were given to the kids to play with. These were, of course, lost. Collections preserved but a portion of the military material produced, especially for a large conflict such as the Civil War. Where is everything?

Pictured below is **the second sword belt plate I found in Ulster County, New York**, well away from the conflict zone of the "Great Rebellion." It is a U.S. sword belt plate from 1851. It became part of the regulation uniform for any federal officer or soldier authorized to carry a sword during the Civil War. Thousands were made in several variations. As rare as the first plate shown is, this 1851 pattern

U.S. sword belt plate type of 1851, recovered in Ulster County, New York

plate is quite common. Comparing the recovered specimen with a close-up of the "Quincy" belt plate, you will notice the faint stain where the German silver wreath had been soldered on and that they are slightly different varieties. However, they are both 1851 pattern belt plates.

The thrill of the discovery of the first artifact spurred me to learn more about it and other military belt plates. When I found the second I recognized its general purpose immediately, and back to the research tools I went. Combined, these and a few other "finds" opened the door for me to an interest in period U.S. military uniforms and accoutrements, so when my cousin showed me "Great-Grandpa's army things," I immediately knew that the belt was of Civil War vintage, but most certainly not that of a bugler! Why would it be with his things?

Next I turned to the buttons from "Quincy's army suit." A handful of obviously Civil War–era military buttons cascaded out of a tattered envelope onto the table and floor. As I hurriedly gathered them up, somewhat embarrassed by my lack of care, I noticed

U.S. sword belt plate type of 1851, from the Adams family collection

a variety of sizes and designs: several small two- and three-piece buttons as well as some that could have been worn by officers, staff, or enlisted men. I counted and rough-sorted them as I picked them up. There were also six coat-sized buttons, each different. So, there were twenty-three in all. The smaller ones were of several different sizes and patterns. I think I started to drool. I had found dozens of similar, mostly U.S., military buttons over the years and knew I was looking at a small treasure. I felt like a tomb raider opening an ancient and dust-covered treasure chest. My cousin said: "Oh my goodness!" It was a polite translation of my exact thoughts. Then my eye caught sight of a palmetto tree on one of the large ones and my hand started to shake. Wasn't it about time for a Sam Adams lager?

After a few deep breaths and some refreshment, I washed my hands, as natural oil and sweat can be detrimental to artifacts. I then examined them and laid all twenty-three of them out in groups.

INVENTORY OF THE "QUINCY" BUTTON COLLECTION

6 coat-sized officer or staff buttons:
1 Rhode Island coat of arms, 2 pc
1 Michigan coat of arms, 3 pc
1 Wisconsin coat of arms, 3 pc
1 Connecticut coat of arms, 2 pc
1 South Carolina, 2 pc (Confederate)
1 U.S. Marines, 2 pc
17 smaller buttons: vest, sleeve, kepi, etc.
6 Massachusetts Volunteer Infantry, 2 different backmarks
2 federal eagle, staff, 3 pc
3 federal eagle, infantry, 2 pc, 2 sizes
6 federal eagle, "I" in shield, infantry, 2 pc, 3 sizes

Twenty-three Civil War–era military buttons from the "Quincy" collection

Several of these State Arms buttons were worthy of separate portraits. A representative of the Massachusetts Volunteer Militia staff button group, whose number indicated that they may have been extras for the original owner's uniform, was nominated for a close-up. It dramatically displays the Massachusetts state military crest: a bent arm holding a broad sword aloft with its blade up.

The six large coat buttons said "button collection" to me. It was apparently a common practice for officers to trade buttons, especially when mustering out at the end of the war. The more numerous and smaller staff buttons suggest "officer." The other federal infantry buttons seem to be a group of leftover button sets.

These and especially the six "I"-in-shield specimens suggest long-term, if not career infantry.

Quincy was a member of a Massachusetts volunteer unit, but he was *not* an officer. Nor would a critically ill soldier worry about such things as button collecting at mustering out. He would just be glad to be alive and going home. The thought came over me: "I don't think these were Quincy's!"

)I(

This is one of three officer's grade vest buttons from the "Quincy" collection. It displays only the military crest of the Massachusetts state arms, surrounded by the state motto. The so-called "broadsword" in the official descripion appears to look more like a saber or a cutlass.

"So who did they belong to?" asked my cousin. "I didn't think the pictures looked like Great-Grandpa! But I thought that all of this was Great-Grandpa's; it came from Grandma Adams." Another doorway to discovery had just appeared.

)I(

With my time at my cousin's place limited, I replaced the buttons in their envelope, all the time eyeing the next artifact, not knowing when I would be able to return and more fully study these items.

The mess kit turned out to be a nice fork and knife in a leather pouch. A quick look revealed two initials: a "B" on one side of the fork's bone handle and a "P" on the other. I felt a dip in my excitement level, thinking out loud: "Who was B. P. or P. B.?" They certainly weren't Quincy's initials. Was this stuff even Quincy's, as the living members of the family had always believed? And if not, who did they belong to and why did the Adams family keep them all these years if they weren't Quincy's? I would ponder this new mystery further when I got home. At the time, I didn't know that my cousin was going to insist that I become the artifacts' new guardian.

)I(

There was one other small, colorful item in the bottom of the box, but it was getting late and traffic was building. Still, I couldn't resist a quick peek at this last item. It revealed the words RE-UNION 35th, REG'T. Hope was rekindled! At that point my cousin offered the collection to me. After a hug and a vow to keep in touch, I hurried home across the Tappan Zee Bridge, to the west side of the majestic Hudson River. My mind was so full of my recent discoveries I barely noticed the Hudson Highlands and Bear Mountain, but soon the growing Catskill Escarpment announced that I was nearing my cozy home in the foothills. By the time I was home I had formulated a plan for the study and preservation of these family treasures. I was going to learn all I could about my great-grandfather, John Quincy Adams.

))((

Back in my study I unpacked and spread out the collection to begin the photographic documentation and evaluation process. I found myself once again being drawn to the buttons. Why a button collection, including none that made sense for Quincy to have? The jacket buttons Quincy is shown wearing in the photographs are hard if not impossible to identify, as with many in photos from the era. Aside from size they are black and white; brass button color was added by retouching with a dot of gold paint. Under the magnifying glass they are just irregular blobs. I wouldn't be able to match any of the buttons with the photos.

Collecting officer's buttons while marching a dozen or more miles a day, setting up and taking down camp, cooking and eating, sleeping on the ground in the rain, in a small canvas tent, while being responsible for sounding perhaps dozens of bugle calls a day doesn't seem like something a nineteen-year-old would be doing. . . . And a Confederate button! Was this a war trophy?

A pair of Confederate States Infantry coat buttons, recovered in Ulster County, New York, by the author, far from the seat of war

As mentioned before, Quincy came home to a loving family. He brought back only a few mementos of his war. The bugle and the journal were clearly his and would be passed down to his offspring. But this stuff, including a war trophy, didn't fit in.

I have found many Civil War–era military artifacts in upstate New York, all well north of the Mason-Dixon Line and far from the seat of war. Civil War soldiers often brought home mementos of this most significant event in their lives. Among them, I am sure, were war trophies that were picked up on the battlefield or taken perhaps from a fallen enemy after a successful engagement, or from a prisoner of war. Like old uniforms and accoutrements, these artifacts were eventually discarded or lost when time had dulled their meaning and the old soldiers died off. This is the only explanation for Confederate items turning up in the yards of old houses and farms in upstate New York. To complete this thought, I offer two short stories that happened to me.

Years ago I belonged to a metal-detecting club in my area. It was customary to bring in items recovered since the previous meeting. One very productive and active member had several items and described one as being part of a Girl Scout belt buckle. This person was more of a treasure hunter and less interested in the historical aspects of his finds. A history-hunting partner (also a Civil War buff and close friend) and I looked down and said almost simultaneously, "How do you get Girl Scout out of 'CS'?" He had found one half of a Confederate States two-piece belt plate. It was immediately raised from just another curio to a "VIA" (very important artifact). We insisted he return to that site and recover the other half.

Several weeks later another cousin was visiting me, from Oregon. He had been a bottle hunter during the urban renewal of Portland in the 1960s and '70s. I secured a site where he could demonstrate how to dig an old privy site for bottles. We found only a few broken bottles, but just before we backfilled the hole I decided to sweep the

A very rare Georgia state seal waist-belt plate, ca. 1850, believed to be a Confederate item and a war trophy as it was recovered in Ulster County, New York, by the author

mound of earth with my metal detector. It immediately sang out "high coin" but with the strength of a very large coin. I had trumped the half-CS plate with a rectangular Georgia state seal belt plate! My cousin immediately yanked it out of my hand and said I'd like a "Civil War thing." Knowing that it was only a casual curiosity to him, but that etiquette would trump my lust to posses this treasure, my heart sank. He picked away at the applied oval seal and a small chunk of bronze flew off. "It's rotted!" he said and thrust it back to me. Talk about mixed emotions: it cost me a little damage, but I'd be taking it to the next meeting of my metal detecting club.

All totaled, I have recovered five Confederate-related artifacts that I believe were war trophies. All of these came from various sites on private property within ten miles or so from my home in upstate New York. They are: the Georgia state seal belt plate, three Confederate "I" buttons from two separate sites, and a spectacular British two-piece, lion-headed, snake-clasped belt plate of a style known to have been brought to the Confederacy via blockade runner. This came from the

British sword belt plate, ca. 1820s, of a type brought via Civil War–era blockade runners to the Confederacy, probably a war trophy. It was recovered in Ulster County, New York, by the author.

middle of an old road along with a dozen or so Civil War tokens and several U.S. half dimes and silver three-cent pieces, all from that era. A period map shows a small building there and we believe the site was that of a tollbooth that operated for a time up until the 1870s. The site has since been destroyed.

A word about ethics: metal detecting or any other disturbance of historical or prehistoric sites or artifacts should never be undertaken without careful consideration. It is completely unethical and almost always illegal on public lands. Collecting on protected sites such as battlefields and state or national parks, may result in the perpetrator being fined or sent to jail, as well as having equipment confiscated. Digging destroys context, the most important part of archaeology. I only search private lands, mostly yards with permission. The types of artifacts I find are usually lost outside of their original-use context and therefore have reduced or inconsequential context. Nonetheless, I keep records of the "finds" in a bound notebook. I use my collections for educational purposes and I am making arrangements for their eventual transfer to responsible persons or the public trust.

Now I can finish my "Great-Grandpa's army stuff" story. Knowledge gained from metal-detected finds and the associated research allowed me to be able to announce: "This stuff didn't belong to Quincy!" With the buttons spread out in front me, I remembered the tattered envelope that the buttons had tumbled out of. Perhaps there was a clue there that was lost to my attention by the glittering brass cascade. I reached into the box of material that my cousin had turned over to me and under a stack of old letters lay a crumpled upside-down envelope, almost as though it were trying to heighten its own drama. When I turned it over my wish was answered. I could immediately see the words: "Buttons from Lewis Hunkins Civil War Army suit."

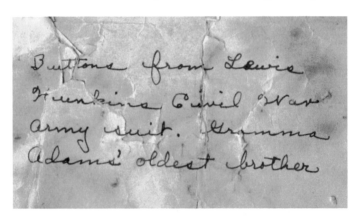

Writing as it appears on the crumpled envelope that held the button collection

I knew they weren't Quincy's! But where had I heard the name Hunkins? Was it from Grandma or my mother? I went back to the genealogy records my mom had bequeathed the family and immediately found a clue. A letter from my mother to her genealogy buddy and sister, Alice, regarding the Hunkins family, was among the papers in her file. The name was familiar but I couldn't recall the connection to the Adams's. An Ensign Sargent Hunkins (I'll explain the spelling of this title in a bit) had married a Sally S. Rowell and had a bunch of kids. Ellena was the only girl. One of her brothers was Ensign Lewis. Could my great-grandmother Eleanor be "Ellena"? Yes! That's where I had heard the name; Ellena would become Quincy's wife after the war. Ellena Hunkins's brother, Ensign Lewis, was Quincy's brother-in-law. These buttons were his! Had he served in the military during the war also? He was born in 1840, right age! And what about his brothers? Horace Mann and Harry Truman, they were the right age also; both James Byron and Carrolus Carrol were too young to have served.

I soon found other notes, charts, and letters that confirm all of this and that Eleanor actually had seven brothers. But the really pertinent and shocking information appeared in a typewritten letter from my mom to one of her sisters updating her genealogy research. Mind you, this was before Ancestry.com and the like.

An excerpt from a letter my mother wrote to her sister Alice, reporting genealogy research on the Hunkins family. "Sin" is presumably a typo ... I hope!

```
Dear Alice:                    Re:  Eleanor (Ellena) W. Hunkins

Haverhill (Mass.) Vital Records to 1850
Vol. I. Births                                m. 9-10-1839
page 179
Hunkins, Ensign Lewis, sin of Ensign S. and
        Sally S (Rowell) born on Nov. 9, 1840

Other children of Ensign S. and Sally S. Hunkins, (still page 179)

        Harry Truman, son of Ensign S. Huckins (carpenter on duplicate)
                and Sally S. (Rowell) June 3, 1844.
        Horace Mann, same parents, born Aug. 23, 1842
        James Byron, same parents, born June 21, 1846.
        Carrolus Carrol, same parents, born Newton, N. H.
                on June 23, 1848
```

It took me awhile to get past some confusion caused by these names, like the "Ensign, Sargent, Officer" thing in the Hunkins genealogy. It turns out that Ensign was a more common first name in the old days, and Sargent wasn't a misspelling. It wasn't meant to be a rank or title, but the mother's maiden name. Three of Quincy's future wife's brothers were also serving in the Union Army during the Civil War. Two of the brothers were killed or somehow died during battles or because of wounds received. All the others except for Ensign Lewis had died young. Quincy would never know Harry Truman Hunkins or Horace Mann Hunkins, but he would surely have known Ensign Lewis, his future brother-in-law. These are all interesting names; it seemed to have been a common practice to name children after famous people. But Harry Truman! ... In 1844?

```
About the Hunkinses.  Ensign Sargent was Grandma's father.  His parents
were Robert and and Betsy (Sargent) Hunkins. (There were very few middle
names given before the Rev. War time.)   Grandma's brother was Ensign
Lewis.  He's the only one of her 7 brothers who lived after age 40.  I be-
lieve he was married twice, his first wife, Annie Blake.  They were Maud
Brown's parents.  The next brother, Horace Mann, I think was  'Rissa Hilton's
father.  He died at 22 in the Battle of the Wilderness.  The next one, Harry
Truman, died at 19, in Baton Rouge, La., also the Civ. War, I think.
James Byron died at 24, Carlos Carroll, 30, just one year to the day before
Dad was born.   There were two Frank Marions, the first d. 2 yrs, the second
19.   Grandma  was almost 80 and Aunt Rhoda died the last, 1939.
Now are you thoroughly mixed up?
```

The excerpt from another of my mother's letters that made me aware of the other Hunkins boys' involvement in the Civil War

An Internet search of Massachusetts soldiers in the Civil War produced twelve Hunkins; among them I found:

Hunkins, E. Lewis   Mass. Officer Inf. U.S.A. and U.S.V. (Miscellaneous Units)

Hunkins, Harry T.   Fiftieth Infantry (Militia)

Hunkins, Horace M.   First Regiment Heavy Artillery

Our Ensign Lewis was an officer, probably a career officer. He served in various Massachusetts units and I am sure that the sword belt was his. Except for sergeants and mounted troopers, enlisted men did not generally carry swords.

The Adams family's eating utensil kit erroneously attributed to Quincy

My attention turned to the "mess kit." Actually, it was a leather belt pouch made specifically to carry a knife and fork. Both were nestled tightly together but not a matched set. The original item was probably sutler supplied, but at some point I believe the fork had been replaced. The leather pouch had no identifying marks, but the bone-handled knife was of Sheffield steel and had "Wm PARNEY/ SHEFFIELD" in scrolls on the blade. There was an obvious "B" crudely carved into the upper side and a "P" (showing) on the underside of the fork's bone handle.

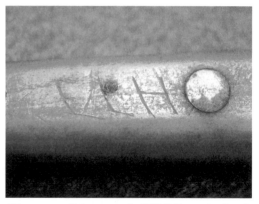

Close-up of the initials "ELH" on the knife handle, evidence that proved ownership by Ensign Lewis Hunkins, Quincy's future brother-in-law.

The final and convincing evidence of ownership came with a closer inspection of the eating utensils. I discovered the carved initials ELH on the knife's bone handle. After the war Quincy would marry a local girl named Ellena Wright Hunkins. Quincy called her Ella, at least in the early years. Ensign Lewis Hunkins, ELH, was Ella's brother. Ensign Lewis would become Quincy's brother-in-law.

This is one of several tintypes in the Adams-Hunkins collection. We believe this is of Ensign Lewis Hunkins, Quincy's future brother-in-law. Quincy is on the right.

Was this entire collection that of Ensign Lewis Hunkins? It made a lot more sense; this is all the kind of stuff that an officer in the Union Army might bring home after the war. The other Hunkins brothers were either killed or died while in uniform. One was, we believe, killed in the Battle of the Wilderness in Virginia, and the other died at Baton Rouge, Louisiana. Neither would ever come home. Records show that they were both buried the same day that they died.

Also in the group was a single well-worn civilian-style stirrup. I had already done most of the deciphering of Quincy's journal and knew that he had not been a member of a mounted troop. In fact, none of the material in this grouping seemed to be that of an infantry bugler. Even the pictures were not of him, save one, and this one showed him seated next to another young man. There was one of another soldier, not Quincy. Were these the Hunkins boys?

Soldiers often marked their personal equipment with painted-on tags. Stencils were often used for this purpose. A tag stencil that was found among Quincy's keepsakes was unquestionably his.

Stencils were a relatively common mail-order or sutler-provided item and there are nice collections displayed in several popular Civil War artifact books. Paint would be placed in the depression and wiped through the stencil, leaving the impression to dry. The process could then be easily repeated on other equipment. Most of

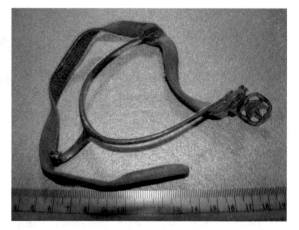

The single, finely made and well worn, civilian-style stirrup found with the Adams-Hunkins group of military material. The iron rowel is all but gone from wear and rust. The scale is metric.

these tags included the person's unit as well as his name. These are occasionally found even today, as they were made of brass, which survives well in the ground. I have looked at several collections and the stencil style in our collection, though less common, matches several. A smaller percentage of those in collections do not show a military unit, just the name, perhaps the thought being that it could still be used after the war.

)I(

The bugle was undeniably Quincy's. I can remember the spectacular Quincy artifacts being in the possession of my grandmother Adams since my earliest memories; this posses-sion was verified by no fewer

Quincy's brass equipment I.D. stencil and the resul-tant tag produced by spreading dark paint through it

than three other cousins. She kept in frequent contact with her father-in-law, John Quincy, all her life and she had lived near him in his senior years. We have a clear chain of custody. The bugle is the centerpiece of the family's history and lore. It and the role it played deserve some special attention here.

Music was very important to the men in the Civil War. It was a pleas-ant escape from the rigors of war. It reminded them of home and loved ones. It filled the boredom of camp life and bonded men together in camaraderie. It encouraged them in battle and explained why they were fighting. It told time and

Troopers and buglers of General Ulysses S. Grant's personal mounted escort. Multiple buglers assured flexibility and redundancy in the transmission of orders. Courtesy of the Library of Congress

signaled what to do and when to do it. The day was ruled by the drumbeat or bugle call, from 5:30 in the morning to 9:15 at night. Every phase of the soldier's life was accompanied by music, and unlike the twentieth century, all the music heard in camp or in the field was live.

The regiment never had a band, although it had attempted to recruit one at Lynnfield. It did have a drum corps, and Company K even had a glee club.

There were band musicians and field musicians. The bands were primarily for parade, ceremony, marching, and "esprit de corps." The bands, if present, were not as tactically important as the field musicians were. Bands may have been used to escort units to and into battle-line formation and probably with large units, right up to the charge in some cases. At that point they were most likely stopped as the din and confusion would soon make them irrelevant. Band musicians would immediately become stretcher-bearers. Field musicians had a tactical function; they were the close-quarter communicators of orders. Early in the conflict buglers were mostly used with mounted units. The five diminutive-appearing buglers shown above are with troopers of General Grant's escort. Infantry units tended to rely on drummers, but a few units had buglers as well. Apparently that number increased as the war went on, since the shrill tones of the bugle could be heard more easily above the roar of battle. In the movies, the hero stands up and yells "Charge!" and instantly thousands of screaming warriors hear him over the absolute din of combat and they all charge forward. In a Civil War battle, with the ear-splitting thunder of thousands of large-caliber, muzzle-loading, black-powder rifles, pistols, and cannons discharging, added to the sound of exploding projectiles, and men and horses tramping, yelling, screaming, and dying, it would have been impossible to count on the Hollywood version of combat communication. The drummers and/or the buglers would have had to be close at hand to hear the officer in charge and be ready to translate verbal commands into audible orders and directions to the troops in combat.

The tactical importance of the field musicians must have made them a desirable target of both the enemy's front line and its sharpshooters; perhaps second only to flag bearers and officers. The short life expectancy of the flag bearer is well documented, and I can't imagine how a drum could even survive a pitched battle. I suspect a bugle would fare somewhat better. And since it is virtually impossible to handle a weapon while playing an instrument, in a charge it must have taken an extra dose of courage to face an enemy bent on killing you, with nothing more than a drum or horn in your hands.

A check of the U.S. War Department's manual titled *The 1863 U.S. Infantry Tactics* revealed a list of no fewer than forty-seven different calls, each call commanding a precise set of steps to be taken. Not only would drummers and/or buglers need to know how to sound each, but the soldiers would need to be able to recognize them immediately.

The only mention of the **positions, or posts, of the musicians**, in the 1863 manual of U.S. infantry tactics is when the ten companies of the regiment are

This fit-looking company of Pennsylvania volunteer infantry with their drummer was one of the units that accompanied the Thirty-Fifth Massachusetts on both the Mud March and at Fredericksburg. Courtesy of the Library of Congress

drawn-up in line of battle and is as follows: "The buglers will be drawn-up in four ranks, and posted twelve paces to the rear of the file closers, the left opposite the centre of the left center company. The senior principal musician will be two paces in front of the field music, and the other two paces to the rear." The regimental line of battle would be two ranks, or lines of men, up to four hundred men across, shoulder to shoulder. This was followed closely (two paces) by a third line made up of various lieutenants and sergeants, called in this case "file-closers." As confusing as this was to me at first, an associated diagram made it quite clear. The field musicians were posted slightly to the left and approximately sixteen paces behind the main battle lines. The regimental band, if there was one, would be drawn up to the rear of these field musicians. The combined calls would be loud enough to be heard by the entire regiment. The post of musicians when the companies were drawn up as a battalion (several companies), was also to the rear centrally. Should the regiment or battalions break into companies, the field musicians would follow their own units. This way orders transmitted from regimental command by regimental buglers would be picked up by the battalions' group of musicians and repeated, and if by company, by the company musicians. Each company was permitted two field musicians. Most buglers had a distinctive musical voice or accent and could be recognized by the other buglers and presumably their own men. Seasoned soldiers could thus recognize their own bugler from those of other companies, even when separated in a forested skirmish line.

GENERAL CALLS

Attention	Retreat	The disperse
The General	Tattoo	Officer's call
The assembly	Taps after (1862)	Breakfast call
To the color	To extinguish lights	Dinner call
The recall	Assembly of the buglers	Sick call
Quick time	Assembly of the guard	Fatigue call
Double quick time	Orders for orderly sergeants	Church call
The charge	For officers to take their places in line after firing	Drill call
The reveille		School call

CALLS FOR SKIRMISHERS

Fix bayonet	Halt	Rise up
Unfix bayonets	By the right flank	Rally by fours
Quick time*	By the left flank	Rally by sections
Double quick time	Commence firing	Rally by platoons
The run	Cease firing	Rally by the reserve
Deploy as skirmishers	Change direction to the right	Rally by the battalion
Forward	Change direction to the left	Assemble on the battalion
In retreat	Lie down	

*This is the only call that is the same on both lists, Double quick time appears on both lists but with different music.

To make it easier to remember all the calls and react before a big mistake could cost a person's life or a regiment in battle, ditties were developed to help learn the calls. Ditties are short singsongs that typically had clever words that related to the meaning of the call. I remember learning several in the Boy Scouts of my era during the half-a-dozen, two-week summer camp sessions as a Scout and two summers as the waterfront director at the Rip Van Winkle Council's Camp Tri-Mount, high in the Catskill Mountains of Greene County, New York. I never knew these as "ditties" but I quickly recalled the ditties for "Reveille," "Mess Call," and "Retreat" some fifty years later and could "mouth toot" them all. I remembered "Taps" as well but was reminded that these were the words to the song "Taps," not necessarily a ditty, although it serves the same purpose. I offer two here as I remember them. "Reveille": *Oh you can't get them up, you can't get them up, you can't get them up in the morning! You can't get them up, you can't get them up, you can't get them up all day!* And for "Mess Call": *Come and get your beans, boys, come and get your beans! Come and get your beans, boys, come and get your beans! Time for chow!* The B.S.A. Bugling Merit Badge called for being able to play sixteen calls; most were the same as in the military of the day.

)|(

Our family tradition is that Quincy was a bugler; two photos exist of him with his bugle. He even mentions practicing on his bugle several times in his journal. However, he also mentions beating out "Reveille" and wanting to get a new drum. It is obvious from his journal that he was a bugler, but there is evidence that he was a drummer on occasion as well.

I suspect that another reason for the increasing use of the bugle was its survivability. Quincy's bugle has multiple impact scars and dents in its nickel-brass body but is still entirely functional. Drums made out of thin pieces of wood and animal hide were larger, clumsier and far more susceptible to damage. I also suspect that the effects of changing humidity and rough treatment would make frequent "tuning" necessary.

This tintype is one of two photos of Quincy with his bugle. He appears to be more serious, seasoned, and fit with his bugle at the ready. The original carrying cord with tassel attached can be seen. We believe this photo was taken during his tour of duty in 1863.

Quincy's bugle from the good side, but still showing many kicks and dents. It appears to conform to U.S. military specifications. The cord was attached in later times for the purpose of hanging on the parlor wall in the Herbert Adams home in Alpine.

A close-up view of Quincy's bugle reveals the manufacturer's medallion: MADE BY - B. G. Wright – BOSTON. B. G. Wright made many other types of brass horns, and seemed to specialize in keyed and valve horns.

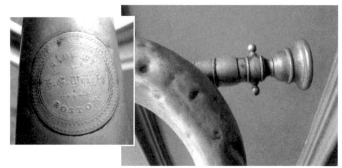

QUINCY'S NEW ADDRESS: THE THIRTY-FIFTH MASSACHUSETTS AND THE NINTH CORPS

"A wandering corps, whose dead lie buried in seven states."
—William F. Fox on the Union Ninth Army Corps,
Regimental Losses in the American Civil War (1861–1865)

Quincy's story is reconstructed on either end of, and throughout his 1863 journal, and presented as a timeline of events based on the history of his regiment, the Thirty-Fifth Massachusetts Volunteer Infantry, and other sources. The most often utilized sources are flagged throughout for the reader's convenience as shown below, depending on the particular source. Those sources were as follows:

9th Corps: The Ninth Corps' history is from The Civil War Archives 1998 –2009, whose source is Regimental Losses in the American Civil War, 1861– 1865 by William F. Fox. ISBN Number: 9781331155263

35th 1: http://www.civilwararchive.com/Unreghst/unmainf3.htm#35th: "35th Regiment Infantry" Original source: "Summary of Service" extracted from *A Compendium of the War of the Rebellion* by Frederick H. Dryer (New York: Thomas Toseloff, 1959).

35th 2: "Thirty-Fifth Regiment Massachusetts Volunteer Infantry – Three Years: Regimental History" from *Massachusetts Soldiers, Sailors, and Marines in the Civil War*, compiled and published by the Massachusetts Adjutant General's Office.

35th 3: "Thirty-Fifth Massachusetts Infantry", an informational sheet provided courtesy of the U.S. Department of the Interior, National Park Service, Antietam Battlefield, Sharpsburg, MD 21782.

35th 4: *History of the Thirty-Fifth Regiment Massachusetts Volunteers, 1862–1865: With a Roster (1884)*, A Committee of the Regimental Association (Boston: Mill, Knight & Co., 1884), reprinted by Kessinger Publishing, Boston 2012 ISBN 0548967377, 2012.

N.G. MAP: "Battlefields of The Civil War with Descriptive Notes", National Geographic Society Map, 1969, Washington, D.C.*

I have placed Quincy's story within a much-generalized timeline of the Civil War's most significant events in order to provide a "global" context. I use several other flags to quickly identify a source or explanation.

Elsewhere in the War: A few selected significant events that took place elsewhere on a given day.

JQA Journal: Verbatim transcription of Quincy's journal of 1863.

Quincy's Words: Selected words from Quincy's journal are explained or expanded upon.

Author's Note: Additional helpful information.

Note: Wording taken directly from all sources preserves source spelling.

April 12, 1861: The Civil War begins with the firing on the Union-held Fort Sumter, South Carolina, by the Confederates.

April 19, 1861: President Lincoln orders the naval blockade of the South and soon after, the capture of the port of New Orleans and the conquest of the Mississippi River. This would eventually cut off the three westernmost seceded states and created a stranglehold on the remainder of the Confederate states.

July 21, 1861: First Bull Run (First Manassas): At Manassas Junction, Virginia, the Confederates, anchored by a little-known brigadier general named Thomas J. Jackson, slow and then stop the Union advance, and then finally turn it into a

---

* **A word about the inserted maps:** Quincy's War will take the reader from the center of the abolition movement, Haverhill Massachusetts, to the hot beds of conflict in the Border States to the western theater of war and into the Deep South. Early-on during the research phase, I realized I would need to have several uncluttered maps to record the movements of Quincy and the Thirty-fifth. I wanted to record not only the locations noted in Quincy's journal and the various regimental histories but also their mode of transportation be it marching, horse or mule-drawn army wagon, steamboat or railroad car. This would allow me to better visualize the great adventure that my Great-grandfather had endured. Professionally made maps were beyond my budget and not in my nature. Using a digital art program I had purchased several years earlier, I was able to draw a base map from which I could generate the regional maps I needed. I have added some notes and placed these five maps strategically though-out his story. They include the place names and transportation modes that make up the odyssey that was Quincy's War.

humiliating rout, the men "flying for dear life" back to Washington. "There stands Jackson: like a stone wall!" exclaimed Confederate General Bernard Bee.

9th Corps: February 1862: The corps that would become the Ninth is "assembled by General Burnside at Newport News, Virginia, from his two brigades from North Carolina and Stevens' division from Hilton Head. The corps consisted of three divisions, under Generals Stevens, Jesse L. Reno, and John G. Parke."

February 17, 1862: Quincy's Eighteenth Birthday

By **April 5, 1862:** "McClellan had landed 121,500 men at Fort Monroe, on the toe of the peninsula between the James and York Rivers, some 70 miles from Richmond. The Peninsular Campaign was under way at last: the slogan of the day was 'On to Richmond!'"

Author's Note: Fort Monroe guarded Hampton Roads and the year-round ice-free harbors of the James River. Hampton Roads referred to the body of water that is the entrance to the bay from the Chesapeake. It was strategically important to both the North and South. Today it also refers to the greater Norfolk metropolitan area as well, and is home to several large military facilities.

May 1862: By Executive Decree Lincoln adds forty-two thousand places to the volunteers, "expanding the regular army by 23,000. On July 22, Congress weighed in by passing legislation for 500,000 more."

N.G. Map: April 6–7, 1862: The Battle of Shiloh, "the first great battle of the war": After a surprise attack by Confederate General Johnston, at Pittsburg Landing on the Tennessee River, "General Grant forced a Confederate withdrawal to Corinth, Mississippi."

N.G. Map: June 25–July 1, 1862: The Seven Days' Battles: The defining battles of General George McClellan's failed Virginia Peninsular Campaign.

9th Corps: July 22, 1862: The Union Ninth Army Corps receives its official number and order of designation and will "distinguish itself in combat in multiple theaters: the Carolinas, Virginia, Kentucky, Tennessee, and Mississippi during the escalating conflict."

Following Quincy's war as his story gradually began to unfold was difficult for me without the repeated use of a 1969 National Geographic map (**N.G. MAP**) that had become a part of my treasured map collection. I was using it so much that for fear of damaging it further, I made enlarged black-and-white copies of various sections for daily use and for tracing Quincy's path with semi-transparent

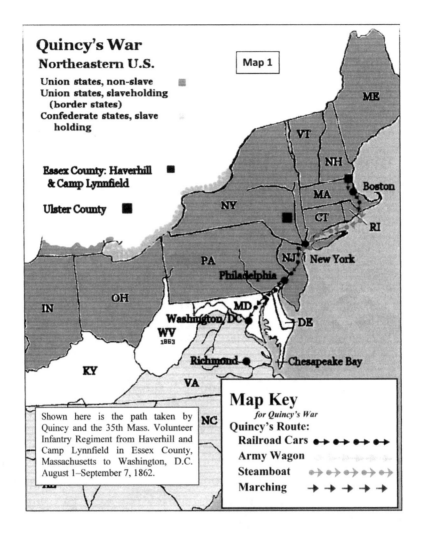

markers. I considered using sections of this map in the book and was told by the National Geographic people that I could obtain licensing—for a price, of course. After consideration of the expense and the fact that there was already a lot of information on the map that didn't directly pertain to Quincy's story, I decided to make my own series of maps. It turned out, however, that my love for maps didn't automatically endow me with mapmaking skills. Using an off-the-shelf picture-editing program, I first traced the outline of the various states from several other maps, scanned it digitally in as a .jpeg file, from this master I was then able to crop and enlarge the sections I would need to produce the six maps I needed to follow Quincy's journey. Finally, I added color and features relative to each phase of his story. It took some trial and error, but I came up with a series of relatively uncluttered, simple-to-read maps.

1862—QUINCY'S WAR BEGINS: SOUTH MOUNTAIN, ANTIETAM, AND FREDERICKSBURG

35th 1: August 1, 1862: The Thirty-Fifth Massachusetts Volunteer Infantry Regiment was "organized in Boston and Chelsea, August 1, 1862, with its' training taking place at Camp Lynnfield. The regiment left the state for Washington, D.C., August 22. Attached to 2nd Brigade, 2nd Division, 9th Army Corps."

35th 2: August 1862: "The 35th Regt. Mass. Vol. Inf. was composed mostly of men enrolled in eastern Massachusetts. It was recruited during July and the early part of August, 1862, and its members were mustered into the service largely between August 9 and 19."

A photograph of the Thirty-Fifth could not be found; pictured here is the Thirty-Fourth Massachusetts at what appears to be near full strength. You may notice the white background of the regimental flag, a type carried early in the war by Massachusetts regiments. Courtesy of the Library of Congress

August 2, 1862: John Quincy Adams is enrolled in the Thirty-Fifth Massachusetts Infantry Regiment.

Know Ye, That John Q. Adams, a Musician of Captain John Y Tobey's Company (G) 35th Regiment of Massachusetts VOLUNTEERS who was enrolled

John Quincy Adams, Thirty-Fifth Massachusetts Volunteer Infantry

on the Second day of August one thousand eight hundred and Sixty-two to serve Three years or during the war, . . . Said John Q Adams was born in Haverhill in the State of Massachusetts, is Eighteen years of age, Five feet Seven & half inches high, Light complexion, Hazel eyes, Dark hair, and by occupation, when enrolled, a Musician.

35th 3: August 22, 1862: "The Regiment was ordered to Washington, D.C., joined to the Second Brigade, Second Division, IX Corps, Army of the Potomac."

35th 2: August 22, 1862: "Under Col. Edward A. Wild the regiment left for the seat of war August 22 reaching Washington on the 24th, (soon to be) attached to the 2nd Brigade, 2nd Division, 9th Army Corps, Army of the Potomac."

August 22, 1862: The Thirty-fifth regiment was outfitted with British-made Enfield rifles. Many of these were later discovered to be defective, fortunately before they were needed in combat, and an exchange took place when the regiment passed through Washington on their way to the front. These rifles fired the relatively new .577 (.58) caliber Minie "ball," a.k.a. three-ring bullet.

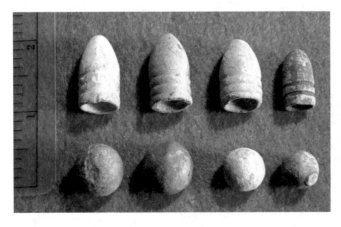

Upper: Three .58- and one .44-caliber Minie-type bullets Lower: Four musket balls: Two .69-caliber (one fired), one .58-caliber, and one .50-caliber

9th Corps: August 28–30, 1862: Second Bull Run (Second Manassas): "At Second Bull Run it [Ninth Corps] fought its first battle as the IX Corps. Only the two divisions of Stevens and Reno were engaged in this action; they numbered 12

regiments and 2 batteries, fewer than 5,000 men. General Reno was in command of both divisions in Burnside's absence. The losses in this small engagement amounted to 204 killed, 1,000 wounded, and 319 missing; total, 1,523. Some of the regiments encountered a severe fire, the 28th Massachusetts losing 234 men." The Thirty-Fifth is not yet attached to the Ninth Corps.

35th 4: September 7, 1862: "Ambulance trains from the front moved towards Washington, with the slow motion that which betokened wounded men within; and stragglers and portions of the Army of the Potomac passed through the camp, notably Meagher's Brigade, of Sumner's Corps, sun-browned heroes of the Peninsula, their clothes weather-stained and worn, flags tattered and ranks thin, telling a tale of hard service, and presenting an appearance which quite shocked us; there were even some wounded men among them. Soon after there came visitors of General Pope's Army of Virginia, with tales of narrow escapes and death of friends in the battles of Groveton, called Second Bull Run. Surely the crises had now come, all the armies were about us, and we were in good position to participate. We gazed over to the city upon the half finished dome of the Capitol, and wondered if it would ever be completed—it looked doubtful. But our short time of preparation was spent; ready or not ready it was time for the Thirty-Fifth to take the field, to keep it until the end."

9th Corps: September 6–12, 1862: "General Reno retained command of the corps on the Maryland Campaign, General Burnside having charge of the right wing of the Army of the Potomac, which was composed of the I and IX Corps. Brig. Gen. Orlando B. Willcox was appointed to the command of Stevens' [First] Division, while the 2nd and 3rd Divisions were commanded, respectively, by Generals Samuel D. Sturgis and Isaac P. Rodman. The command had also been greatly strengthened by the accession of several new regiments, just organized under the recent call for troops, and its four divisions now numbered 29 regiments and 5 batteries, with 13,819 present for duty, including non-combatants." [The Thirty-Fifth Massachusetts was one of these new regiments. Quincy was now a part of the Ninth Corps.]

35th 1: September 6–12, 1862: March into Maryland

35th 2: September 8, 1862: "[The Thirty-Fifth] was assigned to Ferrero's [Second] Brigade, Sturgis' [Second] Division, Reno's [Ninth] Corps."

35th 2: September 14, 1862: "Joining the Army of the Potomac, it [the Thirty-Fifth] took part in the Battle of South Mountain, where Col. Wild lost his left arm."

35th 1: September 14, 1862: Battle of South Mountain, MD.

The Thirty-Fifth, part of the Second Brigade of the Ninth Corps commanded by General Sturgis, was part of the army that fought its way through Fox Gap. Fox Gap was the middle of three defended gaps in South Mountain, a narrow, thirty-some-mile-long wall running north-northeast from the Potomac River and into Pennsylvania. In 2009, my wife, Cathy, and I followed the route of the Thirty-Fifth as best we could, through the gap, discovering along the way the spot where their corps commander, Major General Jesse Reno, was killed. We then proceeded west along the old Sharpsburg Road and down into the northern portal to the Shenandoah Valley toward Sharpsburg, Maryland, as did Quincy and the Thirty-Fifth.

9th Corps: "The Battle of South Mountain was fought wholly by Burnside's two corps, the IX Corps losing 157 killed, 691 wounded, and 41 missing; total, 889. The loss in the I Corps was about the same. General Reno was killed in this action, upon which General Cox succeeded to his command."

This early rendition depicts a Union charge during the Battle of South Mountain, Maryland. The battle was fought in three separate gaps in this fifty-mile-long addendum to the Blue Ridge Mountains, running from the Potomac River north and well into Pennsylvania: Fox Gap, Turner's Gap, and Crampton's Gap. It was Fox Gap through which Quincy and the Thirty-Fifth first tasted combat on September 14, 1862. At this point in the battle Quincy would presumably have been blowing his bugle to relay commands to the troops over the din of battle or manning a stretcher after his unit's direct involvement. Courtesy of the Library of Congress

According to an article in the *Boston Herald* on Friday, September 14, 1928: "South Mountain was the first battle in which the company [Company G, Thirty-Fifth Massachusetts Infantry] was engaged in the Civil War. Three days later the men fought in the famous Battle of Antietam, after which all of the company's [Company G's] 101 men, except eight, were either dead or wounded. . . ."

According to *The Bloodiest Day—The Battle of Antietam*, "The Battle of Antietam was considered the bloodiest single day of the war. More Americans were killed in battle in that one day than in any other single day before or since. Casualties for the Union tallied 2,108 killed, 9,549 wounded, 753 missing and for the Confederates an estimated 2,700 killed, 9,024 wounded, and 2,000 missing."[*]

35th 1: September 16–17, 1862: "*. . . and [the Battle of] Antietam [MD]*"

35th 2: September 17, 1862: ". . . under command of Lieut. Col. Carruth, the regiment lost 214 officers and men, of whom 69 were killed or mortally wounded."

35th 3: Units were often named for their commanding officer. Those associated with the Thirty-Fifth were, in order: Edward A. Wild's Infantry, Sumner Carruth's Infantry, Stephens H. Andrews's Infantry, Sidney Willard's Infantry, and Nathaniel Wale's Infantry.

ONLY SURVIVORS OF CO. G, 35TH MASS DINE TODAY

HAVERHILL, Sept. 13—The three surviving members of company G, 35th Massachusetts infantry, will hold their annual reunion and dinner tomorrow, the anniversary of the battle of South Mountain, at the home of George W. Heath, 28 Moore street. South Mountain was the first battle in which the company was engaged in the civil war. Three days later the men fought in the famous battle of Antietam, after which all of the company's 101 men, except eight, were either dead or wounded.

Boston Herald, **Friday, September 14, 1928**

35th 4: An abridged excerpt of an eyewitness account of the Battle of Antietam appearing in the *History of the Thirty-Fifth Regiment Massachusetts Volunteers, 1862–1865*, is as follows:

> *"Forward!" came the order … "Double Quick!" [W]e rushed out of the little grove Lieutenant Colonel Carruth leading … to the entrance of a stone bridge. … Here was a startling scene of Battle; the 21st Mass. and our Co. A were actively engaged with the enemy posted behind trees. …*

---

[*] Ronald H. Bailey, *The Bloodiest Day—The Battle of Antietam* (Time-Life Education, 1984).

Dead and wounded men in blue lay about, some still tossing and writhing in agony; the bridge was filled with men of the 51st Penn. and 51st NY. The 35th Mass. came into line and joined in the throng hurrying on to the further bank. ... [We] filed into the road to the right, where the two regiments which had preceded us were halted. The line of the regiment was formed quickly and steadily, facing the hill ... then the 35th was ordered up the hill with a promise ... of support advanced up the steep, climbing with difficulty the high rail fences ... reached the brow of the hill. ... Before us, towards Sharpsburg, the enemy were scattering back to their artillery. ... The hostile battery ... opened upon us at once and sent the iron whizzing around us, shells taking effect in [our] companies. ... If support had been up, as promised, the whole could have gone forward, kept the already started enemy upon the go, and, as the zouaves did at a later hour, driven the exposed gunners from their artillery ... for we at least, were green enough to go anywhere without hesitation. ... Our colonel, seeing no support behind him, ordered the regiment to retire under the brow of the hill. ... To stand still upon the exposed hill-top would have been murder. ... Shells hurtled around us as we climbed the fence in retreat; yet many, indignant at the notion of falling back, and fearing more the bayonets of their compatriots while getting over the fence than the missiles of the enemy, waited a bit, until the line had crossed, before following. ... As we thus came back over the fence our batteries, mistaking us for the enemy, commenced firing into us. Colonel Carruth waved his hat, without effect; then his voice rang out, "Unfurl those colors and wave them!" ... We had only the blue and the white flags, no stars and stripes. No more shots came. ...

Author's Note: When I first read that they had only the blue and the white flags, I was unsure just exactly what flags this might be referring to. I was not very knowledgeable regarding unit flags. I knew the regiment did not have its national colors, but presumed that they would have had some sort militia or regimental flag at the time of departure. I contacted the curator at the Commonwealth of Massachusetts, Art Commission, who graciously provided me with pictures and information regarding the unit's flags in their collection. Among the group there were two blue regimental flags and two U.S Stars and Stripes, but no white regimental flag. I would later learn that it had not been returned after the war.

A fifth flag was a faded and tattered banner bearing a very large but very faint red "35" in the center. I wondered if this grayish banner could have originally been white. After further research I learned that this flag was originally blue and the numerals had been gold; the colors had faded so as to leave only the red pigments on the extremely sun-faded material. The black carbon-based pigment of the numbers' shadowing remained near its original appearance. There were no specifications as to size accompanying the photo, but a measurement of what was left of the fringe versus the flag's length indicated that it was a relatively small banner. By tracing the numeral pattern and the flag outline, I was then able to digitally draw a reasonably accurate rendition of what I later learned was a regimental flank-marker flag.

The author's digital rendition of the marker flag of the Thirty-fifth based on the original flag and description now safe in the collection of the Massachusetts Art Commission. The original had apparently sun bleached to an almost white color over the years before modern preservation techniques.

Left: a digital rendition of a white Massachusetts regimental flag by the author. Right: an actual blue U.S. regimental flag carried by the Thirty-fifth Massachusetts Volunteer Infantry Regiment. Courtesy of the Massachusetts Art Commission

The white flag had been the state-issued regimental flag with the Common-wealth of Massachusetts arms on a white field. This was the type that had been presented to the state's regiments upon leaving for the seat of war. It bore the state motto on a ribbon under the blue shield: "*Ense petit placidam sublibertate quitem,*" signifying that we draw the sword to gain enduring peace in a free land."A white state flag is just barely visible in the photograph of the Thirty-Fourth Massachusetts Regiment shown earlier.

The blue flag was a standard U.S. regimental flag with the federal arms over a red ribbon bearing the U.S. motto: *E Pluribus Unum*, meaning "out of many, one indivisible." Two of these flags exist in the collection; one has no apparent wording remaining on its ribbon and the other has "35th. Mass. Vol." visible on the ribbon. The regiment had still not yet received its Stars and Stripes. I decided to digitally create a rendition of what I believe the white state color probably looked like.

))((

At the Antietam National Battlefield Visitor Center, a ranger was most helpful in looking up the Thirty-Fifth's involvement and provided us a lot of information. Actually that is understated: he gave us a stack of info that he had personally collated and highlighted, including the unit's position every half hour of the attack. At the time, we had not learned the unit's history well enough to find the significant spots in our quest on our own. We quickly learned that the unit had a monument at Burnside Bridge. Off we went. Parking and walking to the structure, we couldn't escape the number of markers indicating that something significant had happened here, and that this was hallowed ground. Walking across the lower of the three historic Sharpsburg bridges crossing Antietam Creek, we began looking for the Thirty-Fifth's monument. At the eastern approach to the bridge, I located a polished gray granite monument topped with three granite cannonballs. I was still absorbing the inscriptions on a monument of another regiment we had just passed, when Cathy, standing just behind me, said, "Well, this one says the Eighty-Fifth Massachusetts!" I turned and looked down as we simultaneously exclaimed: "No! *Thirty*-Fifth!" It was like discovering a lost treasure. I spent my career in Outdoor Education and knew well the value of the "discovery" in personalizing learning. For me there is nothing more wonderful in the study of the Civil War, or any "history" for that matter, than connecting on a personal level with the past.

By midday on September 17, 1862, all attempts to secure a Union foothold

---

** *A History of the Thirty-Fifth Regiment Massachusetts Volunteers, 1862–1865*, p. 11.

on the Sharpsburg side of the Rohrbach (lower) Bridge had failed. Several hundred Confederate troops positioned on the hill we had just walked down, were able to concentrate their fire on the congested masses of blue surging across. Finally, it was the turn of the Second Brigade under Brigadier General Edward Ferrero. The "two Fifty-Firsts," from New York and Massachusetts, were able to establish a "beachhead" and plant their colors on the west shore of Antietam Creek. Shortly thereafter it was up to Quincy's regiment, the Thirty-Fifth, closely followed by the Twenty-First Massachusetts, to take the hill and begin the push to Sharpsburg. From that day on the bridge has been known as Burnside Bridge.

The thrill of this "discovery" was euphoric; **Quincy had crossed Burnside Bridge under combat conditions . . . and survived!** For the Thirty-Fifth it was to become a defining moment. We reclosed the bridge with a feeling of respect and awe for what had happened here. We then regained the ridgeline

The monument to the Thirty-fifth Massachusetts at Burnside Bridge reads: "ERECTED BY LIEUT. COL. ALBERT A. POPE, AS A MEMORIAL OF HIS DEAD COMRADES." It bears the badge of the Ninth Corps. Albert Augustus Pope (May 20, 1843–August 10, 1909) was a brevet lieutenant-colonel and after the war founded the Pope Manufacturing Company in 1877.[*]

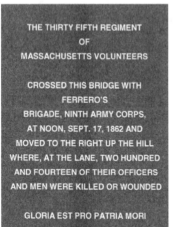

THE THIRTY FIFTH REGIMENT
OF
MASSACHUSETTS VOLUNTEERS

CROSSED THIS BRIDGE WITH
FERRERO'S
BRIGADE, NINTH ARMY CORPS,
AT NOON, SEPT. 17, 1862 AND
MOVED TO THE RIGHT UP THE HILL
WHERE, AT THE LANE, TWO HUNDRED
AND FOURTEEN OF THEIR OFFICERS
AND MEN WERE KILLED OR WOUNDED

GLORIA EST PRO PATRIA MORI

that was the crest of the hill we had just come down with much less worry than had the Thirty-Fifth. It was now their turn to face the awesome maelstrom of Confederate fire from across the fields and behind stone fences. The gray rectangle is a representation of the text inscibed on the granite monument.

Here, I continue to use a scrapbook format to present some of the information we collected on that day regarding this phase of the battle. This is to better share the experience of

---

*** "Brevet Lieutenant-Colonel Albert Augustus Pope, U.S.V.," AllBiographies.com, last accessed October 31, 2015, www.all-biographies.com/soldiers/albert_augustus_pope.htm.

This portrayal by an unknown artist captures the drama of the bridge crossing but inaccurately places General Burnside in the midst. Courtesy of the Library of Congress

U.S.A. Ninth Army Corps
Ferrero's Brigade, Sturgis' Division
Brig. Gen. Edw. Ferro, Commanding
Organization
51st New York, 51st Pennsylvania,
21st and 35 Massachusetts Infantry
September 17, 1862
On the morning of the 17th, Ferrero's Brigade was in position about a half mile northeast of this point on the Rohrback Farm. About 9A.M. it moved to the left and, after several changes of position, was ordered to carry the bridge. The 51st Pennsylvania, 51st New York were formed under the cover of the hill overlooking this point: skirmishers were thrown forward to the stone fence above the bridge and behind the fences and trees along the stream below it; and under cover of the fire from the Federal Artillery, the two regiments charged down the hill, carried the bridge and formed, under cover of the bluff, in the road beyond it. The 35th Massachusetts, closely supported by the 21st Massachusetts, followed and ascended the bluff on the right where, later in the day, it was joined by the remainder of the Brigade and led the advance to the Otto farm lane, where it became severely engaged and lost heavily in killed and wounded.
Late at night the Brigade was relieved by Welsh's Brigade of Wilcox's Division and fell back to the banks of the Antietam.
No100

U.S.A. Ninth Army Corps
Ferrero's Brigade, Sturgis' Division
Brig. Gen. Edw. Ferrero, Commanding
Organization
51st New York, 51st Pennsylvania,
21st and 35 Massachusetts Infantry
September 17, 1862
After Ferrero's Brigade carried the stone bridge it formed under Cover of the high ground north of it. Nagle's Brigade formed on its left. Willcox's, Scammon's, and Rodman's Divisions formed in advance of them and moved on Sharpsburg. On the repulse and retirement of the three Divisions, Ferrero and Nagle advanced to check Confederate pursuit. The left and center of Ferrero's Brigade halted under cover of the crest of the ridge beyond the ravine, the right (35th Massachusetts) continued to advance to Otto's Lane, 270 yards distant, and engaged the Confederates posted on this line and behind the stone walls right and left of it and in the 40 acre cornfield south. The engagement continued into the night, Ferrero's Brigade sustaining much lost, the principle part of which fell to the 35th Massachusetts, which had 214 officers and men killed and wounded. No.68

Above are the stylized texts of the cast iron National Battle field monuments placed on the fields above the bridge.

This period sketch by an unknown artist shows the Confederate line on the crest of the hill. A period photograph exists showing that the openness it portrays to be more accurate than its present day forested appearance. Courtesy of the Library of Congress

discovery of the dramatic events that Quincy and his comrades had endured that day. The shields are representations of the cast iron monuments placed by the National Park Service decades ago on the fields above the bridge, between the crest of the hill and Sharpsburg.

That evening I contemplated the day's discoveries and read the material I had collected at the Visitors Center. I learned that President Lincoln had traveled from Washington to Sharpsburg to meet with General George McClellan during the time of McClellan's lengthy respite after the battle. Lincoln had wanted him to aggressively pursue and crush his foe. After Antietam Lincoln would admonish the general for not immediately pursuing the exhausted Confederate Army. Eventually Lincoln would relieve him of command of the Army of the Potomac and replace him with Ninth Corps commander Ambrose Burnside.

I had vaguely remembered that both my mother and my aunt Barbara had told the story that Quincy had seen President Lincoln at Antietam. It was one of their favorite childhood memories of Grandfather Adams. He would tell and retell the story, highlighting Lincoln's height and how "his feet almost touched the ground when he sat on his horse." I rechecked this story when I visited my aunt in 2011, the last of her generation. She confirmed it!

He may also have seen another man who would be president. William McKinley had served at Antietam as a commissary sergeant in the Twenty-Third Ohio Infantry and would later become the nation's twenty-fifth president. There is a monument at Antietam dedicated in his memory, placed on October 13, 1903, two years after his assassination. Clara Barton, the "angel of the battlefield," also from Massachusetts, had come to Antietam from her work at South Mountain where she brought aid and comfort to the sick and wounded. Had Quincy seen her, or felt her

Lincoln is photographed meeting with General McClellan (third from left) after Antietam, in order to discuss his displeasure with the lack of follow-up action. General George Armstrong Custer is at the far right. Courtesy of the Library of Congress

presence? And who else could he have seen? He must have seen "Little Mac," as the troops called McClellan, and his aide-de-camp, Captain George Armstrong Custer. Custer must have been at McClellan's side. Did he feel the presence of Generals Robert E. Lee or A. P. Hill, who had arrived just in time to reinforce the Confederate right flank against the Ninth Corps? . . . And what of General James Longstreet or the legendary Southern general Thomas "Stonewall" Jackson? They were all there, less than a mile away on the fields above Antietam Creek.

35th 4: "Our first grand review of the Ninth Army Corps was held October 3, in the fields north of our campground [at Antietam] the President, Lincoln himself, riding past, accompanied by Generals McClellan, Burnside and others—all smiling and apparently on the best of terms with each other."

There were also those of Quincy's regiment who became heroes in their own right; there were at least two soldiers of the Thirty-Fifth who were awarded the newly established Medal of Honor. One, Frank M. Whitman, a member of Company G, must have known Quincy. Sadly, one of the other five Adamses in the Thirty-Fifth, private Stephen C. Adams of his own company, was killed and buried on the field.

A year after our expedition to retrace this phase of Quincy's war, I discovered a shoebox file that one of my cousins had inherited. It held several letters written by Quincy to various family members many years after the war. In several of them he wrote about going back to Antietam. This had clearly been a momentous event that would remain with him the rest of his life.

9th Corps: "At Antietam the corps lost 438 killed, 1,796 wounded, and 115 missing; total, 2,349, out of about 8,500 in action. General Rodman was among the mortally wounded. In October, Cox's division returned to West Virginia, whence it had been withdrawn to reinforce Pope, and its brief connection with the corps terminated. This division had made a brilliant record by its gallant services at South Mountain and Antietam."

Militarily Antietam was a draw but strategically it was a Northern victory. The South had shown its full might, yet ultimately had to withdraw. The North was still rolling up its sleeves while struggling with less than brilliant leadership. McClellan had done what he did best, build an army. Now President Lincoln had to find a general who would use it to defeat the South. McClellan was relieved of command and next up was the Ninth Corps' General Burnside.

Lincoln would take this opportunity to play the moral card by announcing his intent to issue **the Emancipation Proclamation**, which would proclaim that all slaves held in portions of states in secession would be freed. All other slaves in states that had not seceded and territory under the control of the Union forces would be freed at the end of the war and Union victory. The timing of this would serve to disrupt and undermine the agricultural base of the Southern economy. Quincy's hometown of Haverhill "was an early advocate for the abolition of slavery and still retains a number of houses which served as stops on the Underground Railroad. In 1834, a branch of the American Anti-Slavery Society was organized in the city. In 1841, citizens from Haverhill petitioned Congress for dissolution of the Union, on the grounds that Northern resources were being used to maintain slavery." Would-be president John Quincy Adams "presented the Haverhill Petition on January 24, 1842. Even though Adams moved that the petition be answered in the negative, an attempt was made to censure him for even presenting the petition."**** After achieving this goal he immediately moved the petition be answered in the negative, as the end of slavery was the issue, not the destruction of the Union. Later in the war, Massachusetts would field several regiments of black soldiers, including the Fifty-Fourth Massachusetts of *Glory* fame.

35th 1: Until October 27, 1862: Duty at Pleasant Valley was, for the most part, rest and recuperation after the Battle of Antietam. The site of this bivouac is not clear. One source puts it about eighteen miles north-northeast of Sharpsburg; another places it between South and Elk Mountains. Yet another shows Elk Ridge Mountain as the location of three contested gaps in the Battle of South Mountain, and Pleasant Valley lying between the South/Elk Mountain range and the Maryland Heights. Suffice it to say this encampment was within a day's march north-northeast of the battlefield. Several of the generals' staff had their wives visit them at this time. For the men it was a bivouac for physical and emotional healing. The Thirty-Fifth had taken a terrible hit; all the companies had men killed. Quincy's Company G had the most, losing thirteen; Company K, twelve; and Company B, eight, including their musician.

35th 4: "We now began to think seriously and estimate the task at hand. We numbered eight or nine officers and three hundred and forty-eight men with

---

**** Amistad Case: 10: National Archives Document Identifier: #301671

the regiment. It was but one month since we left Lynnfield, and two-thirds of our number were gone; at this rate how many would be left at the end of three years? The patriotic fervor which had sustained us did not effervesce so noticeably, but had begun to weaken somewhat in the presence of such stern realities. ... We had seen the slain Confederates on South Mountain and our own

Union officers relaxing with their wives at Pleasant Valley, Maryland. The troops had no such facilities or privileges available to them. Courtesy of the Library of Congress

dead at Antietam, and the grave fact that we had engaged to be, and had become, slayers of our fellowmen stared us in the face. ...Truly, one should not be nurtured among the doves if he is fated to contend with eagles. The depression which usually affects the mind for a time after the excitement of severe combat was upon us."

35th 1: October 27–November 19, 1862: Movement to Falmouth, Va.,

Warrenton, Sulphur Springs, November 15. This movement involved some skirmishing with the enemy.

9th Corps: "Upon the departure of General Cox the command of the corps fell to General Willcox. On November 5, 1862, General Burnside was made commander-in-chief of the Army of the Potomac."

35th 1: December 12–15, 1862: *Battle of Fredericksburg*

35th 2: December 13, 1862: *At Fredericksburg, "it [the Thirty-Fifth] again suffered severely, losing Major Willard, who was in command."*

The newly appointed commander of the Army of the Potomac, General Ambrose Burnside, had sought to capture Fredericksburg, Virginia, an important road, rail, and river junction on the route to Richmond, the capital of the Confederacy. He planned to do this by way of a surprise attack using portable pontoon bridges to cross the Rappahannock before General Lee could react. Within a week of his appointment, Burnside had his plan approved and started south with his three Grand Divisions to Falmouth on the east side of the river, but the late delivery of the bridge sections caused a serious delay. This gave General Lee time to reach the city and deploy the Army of Northern Virginia along the hills to the west above the city. General James Longstreet's corps was directly above the city and Stonewall Jackson's corps along the hills to the south. Confederate snipers hidden in the buildings along the waterfront slowed the deployment of the pontoon bridges. On December 11, 1862, the battle opened with the establishment of a bridgehead, followed by a house-to-house battle with the remaining Confederates sent to delay the Union advancement and provide further time to enhance the already naturally fortified Marye's Heights.

In 2011 my younger brother, Mickey, and I returned to Fredericksburg, approaching from the north as did Quincy, through Falmouth. We turned west and crossed the modern highway bridge over the Rappahannock near the site of three of Burnside's six pontoon bridges, and into the old part of Fredericksburg. The histories indicate that Union General Sturgis and the Second Division of the Ninth Corps had crossed over one of the most northerly pair of the three hastily constructed bridges into the old city proper. The original bridge and the Richmond, Fredericksburg, and Potomac Railroad bridges had been destroyed earlier in defense of the city. The other three pontoon bridges had been built several thousand yards farther south to facilitate the crossing of the Grand Division Left. That night the Union Army continued to crowd into the winter-cold darkness of the semi-abandoned city.

At dawn on Friday the 13, 1862, the Confederate artillery opened a barrage from the high ground to the west and south, on the Union positions in the city. Exploding shells and solid shot turned the city into a deadly shower of stone and brick fragments and burning lumber, through which the Union soldiers, includ-

This diorama in the Fredericksburg National Battlefield Visitor Center is modeled after a period photograph and is an excellent rendition of the burned-out remnants of the city while in Confederate hands.

ing the Thirty-Fifth, advanced. The Thirty-Fifth moved up to and then south-easterly along the principal street to the vicinity of the railroad station, now an Amtrak line.

Following Quincy's route, "Mic" and I proceeded southeast down Princess Anne Street to where we could park the car in the area of the old railroad depot. Here we turned southwest on Lafayette near where General Sturgis's men had crossed and then re-crossed the tracks on their way toward the focal point of the Confederate line. We followed as best we could the footsteps of the Thirty-Fifth through the old town and along the railroad tracks. Here and there protruding from the ground we noticed aged building rubble, including antebellum-style brick fragments, remnants of the destroyed town. Quincy and the Thirty-Fifth would have had to step through and around this rubble on their way to assault the Confederate stronghold. Here the *Regimental History* mentions seeing a regiment moving to their right—"They had green in their caps." They were men of General Meagher's Irish Brigade. Perhaps Quincy, while maneuvering to follow them in the assault, heard their famous battle cry: *Faugh A Ballagh!* Clear the way!

We proceeded up Lafayette Boulevard where we discovered the new Fredericksburg National Battlefield Visitor Center. Typically, the staff was extremely courteous and truly interested in helping us in our quest. They were just as helpful as those at Antietam, providing even more information regarding the involvement of the Thirty-Fifth. The Visitor Center itself stands at the foot of Marye's Heights, just down from the sunken road, which had proved an impenetrable barrier to the many Union attempts to break the Southern lines. I envisioned this area to be just west of the slight depression where the exhausted remnants of each unsuccessful Union assault had sought refuge from the overpowering fire of the enemy. No fewer than five full assaults, each with several waves, had been beaten back by concentrated volleys fired from the sunken road traversing the slope. A partial stone wall running along the road further enhanced it as a readymade fortification. All attempts met with disastrous losses, each made by courageous Union soldiers under the orders of, in my opinion, an absolutely incompetent central command.

Quincy and the Thirty-Fifth were once again in the thick of the battle. After advancing through the town with its many obstacles, the regiment was sent up the slope toward the entrenched Confederates, who where raining murderous fire down upon line after line of Union troops. Theirs was part of the third assault and followed that of the famous Irish Brigade in its disastrous attempt to dislodge the enemy, which like Ferrero's Brigade contained men from Massachusetts, New York, and Pennsylvania. At 2:30 p.m. Ferrero's four "Burnside Bridge" regiments followed.

In words credited to the report of General Sturgis, "Observing this disaster, I ordered General Ferrero to advance with four regiments of this brigade, leaving the fifth to support Dickerson's battery. Under cover of the [Dickerson's] battery, General Ferrero now moved forward . . . completely checking the advance of the foe and forcing him back with heavy loss. As soon as Lt. Dickerson's battery opened, the enemy concentrated a very heavy artillery fire upon it and I was forced . . . to withdraw it."

This indicates a Confederate attempt to advance occurred after the second Union assault but was stopped by Ferrero's four remaining regiments. It also made me wonder if Quincy and the Thirty-Fifth were in this group, or were they the unit left to support Dickerson's battery? General Ferrero commanded the Second Brigade, which consisted of the Thirty-Fifth and the Twenty-First Massachusetts, the Fifty-First New York, the Fifty-First Pennsylvania (all of Antietam's Burnside Bridge fame), and the Eleventh New Hampshire. Here at Fredericksburg, Sturgis sent Brigadier General James Nagle's First Brigade "to the left of Ferrero . . . to open a cross fire," but they had trouble with the terrain, so he had Nagle and the Fifty-First New York move by another route, to support Ferrero's Second Brigade. The Fifty-First New York must have been the regiment that had been supporting Dickerson's Battery; when the battery withdrew the Fifty-First returned for reassignment. This means that the Thirty-Fifth Mass., and presumably Quincy, would have been among the four regiments involved in the direct assault on the Confederate advance mentioned by General Sturgis. After further study this was proved to be correct. The maps of the battle clearly show Sturgis assaulting the sunken road on Marye's Heights. *History of the Thirty-Fifth* vividly describes a horrible scene: "A board fence running at right angles to the front separated the left from the right of the regiment. Through this fence a heavy shot from the right occasionally tore a hole, one of them striking a poor fellow in the bowels cut him nearly in two, tore off the leg of another man and dashed it against the fence, then passed on its way, splattering the men nearby with blood and fragments of flesh."

Quincy will later make reference to this battle in his journal and mention returning to Fredericksburg in several of his letters. It was clearly a significant life experience for him.

In an unedited excerpt from a letter Quincy had written to my mother, his granddaughter, probably about 1924, he writes: "Monday Morning, Dear Ellen. . . I would like to go there the 17th of Sept [anniversary of Antietam] and stop one night and I would like to go back to Fredricksburg, Va., I was there you know in 62 . . . from Grandpa"

9th Corps: According to the Ninth Corps history, the corps suffered a total of 3,238 casualties in these two engagements (Antietam and Fredericksburg). Its losses in killed, wounded, and missing at Fredericksburg alone amounted to over 27 percent of its numbers.

9th Corps: "At Fredericksburg, the casualty lists indicate that the corps took into action 31 regiments and 5 batteries, with a loss of 111 killed, 1,067 wounded, and 152 missing; total, 1,330. Not long after this battle Maj. Gen. John Sedgwick was assigned to the command of the corps, and General Willcox returned to the command of his division, relieving General Burnside."

35th 2: 1862: "It [the Thirty-Fifth] *camped the early part of the winter near Falmouth.*"

Following the pullback to the east side of the Rappahannock, General Burnside declined to go into full winter camp; lightly sheltered from the snow and rain on the muddy east bank of the river, his army suffered discouragement and discomfort. The constant soaking and inactivity caused the men to become ill in increasing numbers and the bugler's sick call was interpreted as "To the doc-tor! To the doc-tor! Come get your pills—of the doc-tor!"

Author's Note: Falmouth, Virginia, was located just north of Fredericksburg and was occupied by federal forces throughout much of 1862 and 1863. Its proximity to the wharves of Belle Plain provided access to the Potomac River via the Potomac Creek, and a rail line northeast to Aquia Creek, which was the river access mentioned in Quincy's journal. The Potomac was the water highway north to Washington and southeast to Chesapeake Bay, the Atlantic, and the Northern industrial centers. Union commanders had located their headquarters southeast of the town during both the Fredericksburg and Chancellorsville Campaigns.

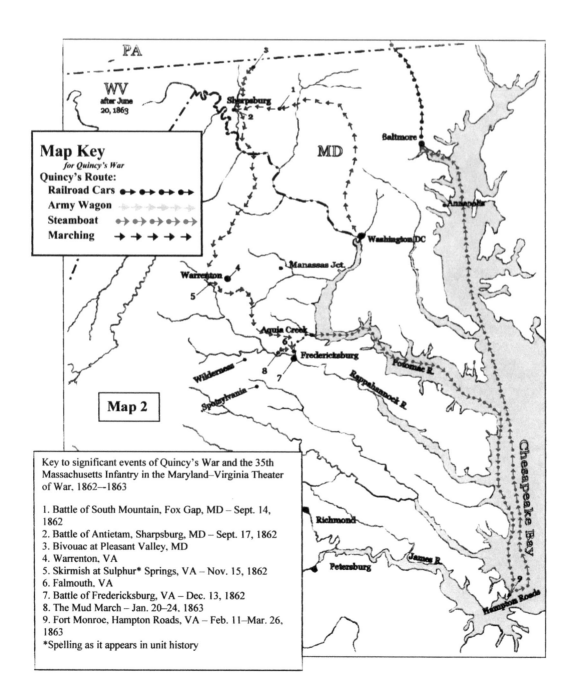

Map Key
for Quincy's War
Quincy's Route:
- **Railroad Cars** ●▸●▸●▸●▸
- **Army Wagon** ●▸●▸●▸●▸
- **Steamboat** ●▸●▸●▸●▸●▸
- **Marching** →→→→→

Map 2

Key to significant events of Quincy's War and the 35th Massachusetts Infantry in the Maryland–Virginia Theater of War, 1862–1863

1. Battle of South Mountain, Fox Gap, MD – Sept. 14, 1862
2. Battle of Antietam, Sharpsburg, MD – Sept. 17, 1862
3. Bivouac at Pleasant Valley, MD
4. Warrenton, VA
5. Skirmish at Sulphur* Springs, VA – Nov. 15, 1862
6. Falmouth, VA
7. Battle of Fredericksburg, VA – Dec. 13, 1862
8. The Mud March – Jan. 20–24, 1863
9. Fort Monroe, Hampton Roads, VA – Feb. 11–Mar. 26, 1863
*Spelling as it appears in unit history

1863—QUINCY'S JOURNAL: VICKSBURG, JACKSON, CAMPBELL'S STATION, AND KNOXVILLE

At this point Quincy's journal of 1863 becomes the primary framework for our time line. I have displayed his journal entries, which were written in script, in italics to distinguish them from other information. I note journal page numbers, dates, and entries if present and a "No Entries" if there are none. The sources of other information are tagged for easy source identification. I include annotations in the journal section with information relative to Quincy's entry or events that were significant to the greater story of the Civil War. This is meant to provide a contextual benefit for the reader. Quincy's words, grammar, spelling, and syntax are shown as close as possible to their appearance in his journal. Quincy's handwriting varies depending on many factors including fatigue, lighting, and weather conditions. Keeping a journal at the age of nineteen, living in a cold, wet canvas tent in an 1863 war environment, writing with primitive writing utensils, often with freezing ink, on damp paper, probably by candlelight and with a grammar school education, was a feat in itself. In several cases where I was not reasonably sure of a word, I used the best probable word followed by a question mark in parentheses (?). Inserted words are enclosed in brackets [ ] and unreadable letters are indicated with slashes ///. I have also continued to follow the various histories of his regiment, the Thirty-Fifth Massachusetts, and the Ninth Corps, of which the Thirty-Fifth was a part throughout the remainder of this book.

Quincy seems to have received the "diary" early in February, as the first entry was the fifth of that month. Three pages, from pages 25 through 30, which contained January 1 through February 18, are missing. They were torn out together. The remains of the torn-out sheets may be seen in the picture entitled "Presidents of the United States."

There were seven separate sheets included loose in Quincy's journal book. These were curious as they included wording and dates already in the journal. No living relative knew why these aged pages were included. At first, I thought perhaps Quincy had started keeping a journal on separate sheets of paper before he had received the book and then copied them into the journal when he received it. Perhaps he had started to transcribe the seven separate pages on the first few pages of the book, then realizing that the dates didn't match, tore them out and started on the correct date. This would explain the torn-out pages. This would also prove to be a rather elementary mistake on my part. The sheet paper, while old and yellowed, was not as antique as that of the journal. The wording on the sheets matched almost

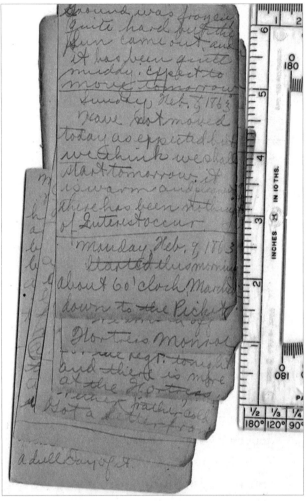

The seven separate pages shown here with scale were written on both sides in pencil.

verbatim that of the journal, but differed in a few ways that this theory could not explain. Sentences started with capital letters and ended with periods, something Quincy rarely bothered with, and some misspelled journal words were spelled correctly on the sheets. Had Quincy forgotten proper sentence structure and how to spell in a few weeks? Finally, the vertical axis of the handwriting and other major differences in its appearance were now obvious to me. I was glad that Sherlock Holmes wasn't looking over my shoulder when I finally noticed it; I'd be headed back to detective school. The only reasonable explanation is that someone had attempted to make a handwritten transcription of the journal many years ago, perhaps one of the granddaughters.

PRESIDENTS OF THE UNITED STATES.

NAMES.	When Born.	Inaugurated.	Continuance in office.	Died.	Native of
George Washington.	Feb. 22, 1732..	April 3, 1789..	8 years	Dec. 14, 1799.	Virginia.
John Adams........	Oct. 19, 1785..	March 4, 1797..	4 "	July 4, 1826..	Mass.
Thomas Jefferson...	April 2, 1743..	" 4, 1801..	8 "	July 4, 1826..	Virginia.
James Madison......	March 16, 1751.	" 4, 1809..	8 "	June 28, 1886	"
James Monroe......	April 2, 1759..	" 4, 1817..	8 "	July 4, 1831..	"
John Quincy Adams	July 11, 1767..	" 4, 1825..	4 "	Feb. 23, 1848.	Mass.
Andrew Jackson....	March 15, 1767	" 4, 1829..	8 "	June 8, 1845..	S. Carolina.
Martin Van Buren..	Decem. 5, 1782	" 4, 1837..	4 "	....	New York.
William H. Harrison	Feb. 9, 1773...	" 4, 1841..	1 month....	April 4, 1841.	Virginia.
John Tyler	Mar. 20, 1790..	Succeeded to the office of President......	3 years and 11 months	....	"
James K. Polk......	Nov. 2, 1795..	March 4, 1845..	4 years......	June 15, 1849	N. Carolina.
Zachary Taylor.	Nov. 24, 1790..	" 4, 1849..	1 yr. 4 mos..	July 9, 1850..	Virginia.
Millard Fillmore.....	May 7, 1800...	Succeeded to the office of President......	2 years and 8 months.	....	New York.
Franklin Pierce....	Nov. 23, 1804..	March 4, 1853..	4 years......	....	New Hamp.
James Buchanan....	April 23, 1791.	" 4, 1857..	4 "	....	Penn.
Abraham Lincoln...	Feb. 12, 1809..	" 4, 1861..	....	....	Kentucky.

January,

Page 24 of the Almanac portion of the journal just happens to show the presidents of the United States, including John Adams, and Quincy's namesake, John Quincy Adams. The torn edges of pages 25 through 30, which were ripped out together, can be seen (arrow).

JQA Journal: (pp. 1–24) Almanac with printed list entitled: "PRESIDENTS OF THE UNITED STATES" on p. 24

JQA Journal: (pp. 25–30)

January 1–18, 1863: Pages Missing

Author's Note: These pages were torn out of the book and are lost.

Elsewhere in the War: December 31–January 2, 1862–3: Battle of Stones River (Murfreesboro), Tennessee: This battle provided a much-needed and strategically important Union victory and secured control of Kentucky.

January 1, 1863: The Emancipation Proclamation takes effect.

JQA Journal: (pp. 31–35)

January 19–31, 1863: No Entries

February 1–2, 1863: No Entries

Author's Note: Pages one through twenty-four contain front matter and almanac material, January one through eighteen have been torn out, January 19 through February 2 exist but with no entries. Apparently Quincy did not receive the book from home until near the end of January. Perhaps it was waiting for him when he returned from the Mud March. Quincy may have begun recording February's events on the January sheets, then realizing his error, tore them out of the book and started on the correct pages.

35th 1: January 20–24, 1863: "Mud March"

January 20, 1863: General Burnside and the Army of the Potomac left their midwinter camp at Falmouth, Virginia, and marched west toward Bank's Ford. Here Burnside would cross the Rappahannock River and try once again to defeat General Lee's Confederate Army by approaching Fredericksburg from the west, but the winter's snow and ice turned to rain and mud. The gambit failed and the campaign was forfeited. Burnside was forced to return to Falmouth, with his exhausted army. Now at least the army could dig in and try to keep warm.

While this etching on wood by A. R. Ward, which appeared in *Harper's Weekly*, **was not identified as specifically being the Mud March, it more than adequately conveys the misery of such an undertaking. Courtesy of the Library of Congress**

January 25, 1863: General Burnside's repeated failure to reach Richmond, the capital of the Confederacy, by way of Fredericksburg, was perhaps the "final straw." President Lincoln removed him from command of the Army of the Potomac and replaced him with "Fighting Joe" Hooker.

35th 1: 1863: "At Falmouth, (Va.) until February 19"

Author's Note: According to Quincy's journal and *Massachusetts Soldier*, this should be February 9, not 19.

JQA Journal: (p. 36)

February 3–4, 1863: No Entries

Thursday, February 5, 1863: *received a box from Home to day is stiring and cold got a Letter from Home to day got my boots to and am very much pleased with them*

Author's Note: Quincy typically uses "to day" rather than "today," as do other writers of that time.

Quincy's Words:

got my boots: Union soldiers were supposed to receive at least several pairs of new boots a year from the government, but they probably didn't. It is unclear whether these boots were from home or Government Issue. Footwear wore out quickly in the infantry and could possibly be replaced by way of sutler or battlefield salvage. The Thirty-Fifth was apparently issued brogans when heading west. Brogans were a cross between a boot and a moccasin.

35th 4: "An army brogan, made in imitation of a moccasin for use on soft prairie land, was not stiff enough in the sole for such work, [and] gave out after a few days' wear."

JQA Journal: (p. 37)

Friday, February 6, 1863: *to day is fair I have been out practicing on my Bugle it talked strongly of that we are going down to North Carolina*

These are the boots, called "brogans," of an exhausted member of the 150th New York reenactors. They are being displayed from two angles and are accurate except possibly for the clean socks. All reenactors' photos were taken by the author at Ashokan in 2011.

Quincy's Words:

I have been out practicing on my bugle, it talked strongly that we are going down to North Carolina: This is one of my favorite lines from the journal. To me it shows a youthful Quincy ready for the great adventure that the camp scuttlebutt proclaims. It may also provide a hint as to the thrust southward that the Union high command may have been considering.

35th 4: "The fate of the [Ninth] corps was to be sent about wherever there was a call for assistance; and it soon, very naturally, acquired the name of 'The Big Class in Geography.' Appearances were now in favor of its return to North Carolina, and the first movement was in that direction."

Saturday, February 7, 1863: *it was rather cold this morning the Ground was frozen quite hard but the sun came out and it has been quite muddy expect to move tomorrow*

Sunday, February 8, 1863: *have not moved today as expected but we think we shall start tomorrow it is warm and pleasant There has been nothing of interest occur*

JQA Journal: (p. 38)

Monday, February 9, 1863: *started the morning about 6 oclock marched down to the Pickets took the Cars Acquia Creek Arrived there about 11AM went on board the Steamer Louisiana where we now are*

35th 2: "On February 9, 1863 it [the Thirty-Fifth] was transferred to Newport News, Va."

Tuesday, February 10, 1863: *started this morning the day has been very warm and pleasant but we are now out on the Chesapeak Bay the sky is cloudy and it is quite cool.*

Wednesday, February 11, 1863: *we arrived off Fortress Monroe Staid there a short time. expected to land but did not. started for Newport News. where we now are The Day has not been so warm as it was yesterday. it looks like Rain*

Quincy's Words:

Pickets: Pickets were the outpost guards set up around a military encampment, especially in hostile territory, to warn off intruders or of a surprise attack.

Cars to "Acquia" Creek: The cars were railroad cars. There was already a branch of the Fredericksburg & Richmond Railroad running from Fredericksburg to Aquia (not Acquia) Creek landing, on the Potomac and thus Chesapeake Bay. After exchanging hands several times, it was under Union control in February 1863, and it became a logistical supply point for Burnside's army.

Steamer Louisiana: A steam-powered vessel with side-wheel paddles. It also towed two troop-filled schooners on this trip.

Fortress Monroe: The coastal defense fort at the easternmost point of the Virginia peninsula.

The landing on Aquia Creek showing the railroad terminus, the docks, and the masts of schooners, ca. 1864. Courtesy of the Library of Congress

The massive sally port of Fortress Monroe guarding the entrance to Hampton Roads, Virginia. This fort remained in Northern hands throughout the war. Courtesy of the Library of Congress

JQA Journal: (p. 39)

Thursday, February 12, 1863: *the Weather has been quite warm here to day, for Virginia There was a lot of Boxes for the Regt to night and there is more at the fortress we have a Ration of soft Bread to night expect to have it right along.*

Wednesday, February 13, 1863: *got a Letter from Home dated the 4th of this month we have lived very well to day the Wether has been pleasant we are going to have boxes every day like very well*

Thursday, February 14, 1863: *Wether rather cold got a letter from Home dated the 8th of this month been out bugling to Day* <u>considerable</u> *getting along well.*

Quincy's Words:

Virginia: This word was very hard to read but since he was at Fort Monroe, Virginia, I compared the pattern of the long strokes of the "V" and "g" and they fit.

a lot of Boxes: These appear to be food ration boxes. Typical rations for the infantry soldier varied for camping and marching, but were supposed to consist of: meat (usually salt, pork, or beef), hard bread, beans, potatoes, some dried fruits and vegetables, basic condiments, and of course coffee, even instant coffee, in a pasty mixture with sugar and cream already added. The unit history often mentions salt, pork, bacon, and coffee.

Ration of soft Bread: Soft bread must be relatively fresh. Hard bread, a.k.a. hardtack, was a plain flour-and-water biscuit approximately three inches square by half an inch thick. They were often called "worm castles" by the men, but they would last until consumed by men or insect larvae. A ration was about ten a day. The Napoleonic dictum that "an army marches on its stomach" is true here in the Union Army as well, and it was the Commissary Department whose responsibility it was to make sure they could march.

got a Letter from Home dated the 4th (and 8th) of this month: Quincy seems to be gauging how long it takes a letter from home to find him, in this case nine and six days respectively. The number of times he records writing and receiving mail in his journal reveals the significance of this connection for the young soldier far from home.

been out bugling to Day . . . : Quincy may have been exposed to brass horns with valves such as the coronet in his musical training. However, the military bugle, while very simple in structure and easy to maintain, was not an everyday civilian instrument and I am told not the easiest to play. I am not musically inclined but I have tried both and was able to play a simple but recognizable tune ("Mary Had a Little Lamb," I think) on a trumpet but NOT on the bugle.

JQA Journal: (pp. 40–41)

February 15–20, 1863: No Entries

35th 4: February 19, 1863: "At first we had our low shelter tents only, but, on the nineteenth, 'A' tents were distributed one to every five of the men, which made extremely close quarters. Some of these tents, owing to the increasing scarcity of cotton, were made entirely of hemp cloth, and were about as useful as sieves for keeping out rain. . . ."

JQA Journal: (p. 42)

Saturday, February 21, 1863: *Wether has been fair it looks like rain our Lieu't Col and Adjt returned this forenoon there was much cheer-ing the Band serenaded him to night,*

Sunday, February 22, 1863: *Cold and stormy been snow-ing hard all Day, had to lay in our Tents all of the time no mail to night on account of the Storm it has mosty stoped rain-ing and snowing now*

Monday, February 23, 1863: *rather cold this morning Lieu't Col Carruth took command of the Regt at Dress Parade to night and Nat Wales took his old Place as Adjt seems like old time.*

Quincy's Words:

Lieu't Col Carruth: Lieutenant Colonel Sumner Carruth of Chelsea, Massachusetts, commander of the regiment, was "commissioned on August 20, 1862, at the age of 27 as a Major. He was a field and staff officer in the 35th Regiment, Massachusetts Infantry [three years]; commissioned a Lieut. Colonel, Aug. 27, 1862; he was wounded Sept. 17, 1862, in Antietam, Md.; prisoner near Fauquier White Sulphur Springs, Va., on Nov. 14, 1862; paroled; exchanged and returned to duty, Feb. 21, 1863; comm. Colonel, April 25, 1863; must. May 1, 1863; must. out June 9, 1865, as Colonel. Brevet Brig. General U. S. Vols., to date April 2, 1865."[*]

Nat Wales: Major Nathaniel Wales of Dorchester, Massachusetts, was "commissioned 1st Lieutenant and Adjutant age 19. Field and Staff July 15, 1862; 35th

---

[*] *Massachusetts Soldiers, Sailors, and Marines in the Civil War Vol. III*, Adjutant General's Office Massachusetts, (Norwood, MA: Norwood Press, 1932).

Infantry – 3 Years must. Aug. 21, 1862; wounded Sept. 17, 1862, at Antietam, Md; prisoner near Fauquier White Sulphur Springs, Va., Nov. 14, 1862;
paroled, exchanged and returned to duty, Feb. 21, 1863; comm. Major, April
25, 1863; must. Aug. 25, 1863; resigned and discharged. May 9, 1864. Brevet
Lieut. Colonel and Colonel U. S. Vols., to date March 13, 1865."[**]

Adjt.: Abbreviation for adjutant, a military staff officer who assists the
commanding officer.

Band: Many regiments had a band consisting of a drum group, fifes, coronets,
and over-the-shoulder brass instruments such as saxhorns and tubas.

JQA Journal: (p. 43)

Tuesday, February 24, 1863: *warm and pleasant had a Brigade Drill this Afternoon are going to have a lot of Drums in about a Week and I am going to take one.*

Wednesday, February 25, 1863: *been a splendid Day to Day been out on Review
the whole Corps was reviewed am up in Mr Broad-bents tent the Brigade ~~Brigade,
Bugler~~*

Thursday, February 26, 1863: *been Fair Wether to day been singing to night down
in Syman Edgerly's tent had a fine sing   there is any Quantity of Ball play-ing
here now*

Quincy's Words:

Brigade Drill: A brigade was typically made up of four regiments, often from
the same state. Nominally at least four thousand men, but attrition lowered the
numbers since casualties often were not replaced by new recruits, especially in
the Union Army. A veteran brigade more likely had closer to half that number
or sometimes even less.

Drums I am going to take one: This is the first evidence that Quincy was also
interested in playing the drum. He may have often doubled as a drummer.

whole Corps: [Ninth Corps] Ideally a corps was ten regiments with ten companies
each, or ten thousand men. They were rarely at full strength after the first days.

[**] *Massachusetts Soldiers, Sailors, and Marines in the Civil War Vol. III*, Adjutant
General's Office Massachusetts, (Norwood, MA: Norwood Press, 1932).

Mr Broad-bent's tent: Leonard Boardman, of Waltham, Massachusetts, is listed in the roster as a fifer but apparently served as the bugler of the Second Brigade, Second Division, Ninth Corps. He was a spinner by profession. He enlisted June 8, 1862, at age twenty-one, and joined the Thirty-Fifth Massachusetts Infantry Regiment, Company D, on August 16, 1862. His rank at enlistment: Musician (fifer). He survived the war, possibly wounded, and mustered out on June 9, 1865, at Alexandria, Virginia.***

ball playing: Most likely baseball. Before the Civil War, a baseball-like game had been around a long time, with regional variants. Apparently in New England it was even called "The Massachusetts Game." This became a popular slack-time activity of the soldiers during the war and would survive to become a national pastime. It is a myth that Abner Doubleday invented the game.

Syman Edgerly's tent: This person could not be located in the regimental roster. His first name is probably Simon and he was most likely a musician in another regiment of the brigade.

35th 4: February 26, 1863: "…rumor took the incredible shape that the ninth Corps was to be sent to the Department of the Ohio, it seemed a travesty of Greeley's 'Go West, young man!'… on the twenty-sixth we were off…."

A regimental band identified as that of the Eighth New York State Volunteers, July 1861, is apparently from Elmira, New York. The larger brass horns project the sound back over the shoulders of the musicians toward the marching troops. Modern band instruments project forward toward the audience. Coincidentally, Quincy would spend his senior years in the Elmira, New York, area. Courtesy of the Library of Congress

JQA Journal: (p. 44)

Friday, February 27, 1863: *been cloudy but not much Rain now going to drill in skirmishing to fort Lieut fi commanding our Co concluded he would not*

*** https://archive.org/details/massachusetts, 37–38, "Mr. Boardman,"

Saturday, February 28, 1863: *Wether fair and warm got 2 Letters to night one from Home and one from W////'s they are having a Dance out on the Parade Ground first time I heard a Violin* [inserted above the last four words] *for a long time*

Sunday, March 1, 1863: *has been fair Wether to day had been out practicing on on the Bugle and came back to Camp when who should I see but our Lieutenant from / l/hsbrug/ i god letter and a Poc/y*

Quincy's Words:

***drill in skirmishing*:** Skirmishing is an important military maneuver that requires a smaller group of soldiers, for instance a company or two, to spread out in advance or around a larger group like a regiment to forewarn of, or disrupt the enemy upon initial contact.

to fort . . . : At first I thought that this might say "to fort Saint Pepi.," or "Phillip." There was a Fort Saint Phillip, but that was on the Mississippi River in Louisiana. "Pipi" might have been a local name. I now take it to be: . . . skirmishing "to [the] fort. Lieut. Pipi commanding our Co. [Company]." The fort would have been at or near Newport News and was probably Fort Monroe on the southernmost point of the Virginia Peninsula. The Virginia Peninsula was the site of McClellan's first attempt to capture the Confederate capital of Richmond.

Author's Note: March 1: The last sentence was so faded it was virtually unreadable; scanning, enlarging, and enhancing helped considerably. My transcription in script is below; ( ) indicate guesses, / unidentified letters. I present it here for the experience of the reader.

. . . should I see but (our Lieutenant) from / l/hebrug/ (and) a letter and a Pocly

JQA Journal: (p. 45)

Monday, March 2, 1863: *went down n into the fortifications to Day and bought some writing Paper and answered Mary's Letter ~~last ahysh~~ that I got last night*

Tuesday, March 3, 1863: *been very warm to day but came up cold at night wrote a letter Home to day been out skirmishing to day to day*

Wednesday, March 4, 1863: *been very cold to day Leiut Washburn Takes command of our Co and Nent takes his old place as Adjt got two letters to night one from Home and the other from Mary*

Quincy's Words:

went down into the fortifications: This was the same "fort" mentioned on February 27 and was apparently the location of the regimental sutler. A sutler was a trader authorized to sell sundry supplies to the men of the regiment.

Nat takes his old place as Adjt.: This refers to Nathaniel Wales. Adjutants were typically captains or lieutenants who were assigned to assist commanding officers.

writing and letters: Pictured below is a reenactors-grade officers' writing case with ink, fountain, or bladder pen, pencil, and goose quill pen with metal point. Quincy may have used a bladder pen at least part of the time as well as a straight pen and a pencil. Perhaps he even had one of the many early mechanical pencils available from the regimental sutler.

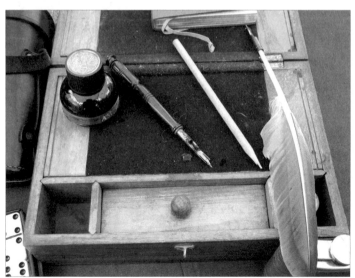

Officer-grade writing case, which was on display at the Ashokan Center Civil War Days

JQA Journal: (p. 46)

Thursday, March 5, 1863: *Wether been cold. got a letter from Charley Steuart to night Steuart and my self have been taking a little walk to night up by the guard tent*

Friday, March 6, 1863: *been warmer to day The drum Corps have been out practicing on their new Drums*

Saturday, March 7, 1863: *been showery to day rains few minutes had a haversack this Afternoon it is raining quite hard now looks as though it would rain all night*

Quincy's Words:

guard tent: It is not clear whether this is a tent for the camp guard or a tent for guarded prisoners of minor offense.

drum corps . . . new drums: An accurate portrayal of a drum corps drummer with his new drum is on the following page.

haversack: (Pictured below) A haversack was the standard bag for food rations. They were commonly made of white canvas or black oilcloth. They were slightly larger than 12" x 12", and were carried over the right shoulder by a strap. They were originally made to be waterproof but lost that ability and would become fouled from carrying raw food.

This captain of the 150th New York (reenactors) is an accurate portrayal of a Union line officer.

JQA Journal: (p. 47)

Sunday, March 8, 1863: *rained last night been out on Inspection to day going to have a general Inspection tomorrow thou likely to have had their's to day*

Monday, March 9, 1863: *been warm and pleasant out been out on Inspection Regt made a fine appearance.*

A canteen, cup, and haversack filled with the daily ration of food hang in the opening of the "dog tent," along with the soldier's rifled musket ready for the day's march to begin.

Elsewhere in the War: On this day (March ninth), in 1862, the famous first clash of ironclad naval vessels, **the USS Monitor and the CSS Virginia (Merrimac)** took place off Fortress Monroe where Quincy had penned his February 11 journal entry.

Veteran drummer Bill Frueh of the Seventy-Seventh New York Volunteer Regiment is captured by the camera wearing his musician's dress coat and trying out a new drum at the Ashokan Civil War Days.

Tuesday, March 10, 1863: *been raining and cold had to stay in the tent all Day*

Quincy's Words:

inspection: Unit inspections were a frequent part of army life. Their purpose was to check and maintain the unit's readiness for action.

had to stay in the tent all day: Prior to February 9, Quincy would have just had a single canvas shelter. The dog tent was formed by two one-man shelters, some-

Pictured here is an inspection of a battle-hardened and much-depleted company of reenactors from the 150th New York Infantry Regiment, at the Civil War Days, 2011, Ashokan Center, in Ulster County, New York.

times called shelter-halves, buttoned together to form a crude tent "just big enough for a dog." Each end was still open to the weather, therefore providing the barest of protection from the rain and wind. Sometimes the men would button four or six shelters together for more living space. By this time the regiment had been issued "A," or wedge tents. Slightly bigger than the dog tent, they were expected to hold four or even five men and required wagon transportation. However, since they were still camped in a more permanent site outside Fort Monroe, they could have been in larger tents. Several different types of tents can be seen elsewhere within these pages, including the larger walled tents and the conical Sibley's tent, which could hold as many as twenty men sleeping like the spokes of a wagon wheel with their feet in. Stories exist claiming that when crowded in, the men had to sleep all facing the same direction like stacked spoons. When one needed to roll over he would yell "spoon" and all would roll at once. Sibley's tents can be seen behind the picture of the Thirty-Fourth Massachusetts on the first page of this chapter. Walled tents were perhaps the most comfortable, but were used for longer-term camping or when the supply wagons could bring them to the troops. Hospital tents were still-larger walled tents.

JQA Journal: (pp. 48–49)

March 11–15, 1863: No Entries

Monday, March 16, 1863: *cold and rainy been out practicing and the cold Wind made my lip quite sore*

9th Corps: "General Burnside had been assigned to the command of the Department of Ohio, a district which included Kentucky and East Tennes-

The dog tent was light and easily carried by the soldier. It was formed by combining two individual shelter-halves. Shown is a dog tent at the encampment of the 150th New York.

see. He obtained permission for the transfer of his old corps to this field of operations, and so, on the 19th of March, 1863, General Parke was ordered to proceed there with his two remaining divisions, Willcox's and Sturgis'. Just prior to the departure from Virginia, General Sturgis was relieved, and General Robert B. Potter was assigned to the command of the Second Division. The Ninth Corps was stationed in Kentucky for two months, during which it served as an army of occupation, its pleasant quarters and light duty making it the most enjoyable period within its experience."

JQA Journal: (p. 50)

Tuesday, March 17, 1863: *been warm and fair our knapsacks came from Washington where they have been stored ever since we left Arlington Heights*

Wednesday, March 18, 1863: *the knapsacks are delivered out to day got my dress Coat and everything all right*

Thursday, March 19, 1863: *been hailing and snowing all day and there is undescribable Snow on the Ground to night cold and disagree-able*

Quincy's Words:

knapsacks: There were many different types of knapsacks issued to Union troops made of various materials such as painted canvas, enameled leather, hair-covered calfskin, wood, and even gutta-percha. Most resembled a black rectangular box held tightly to the back. Most had problems and were uncomfortable to carry. Each soldier would also be carrying his own ammunition, weapon, extra clothes, blanket, knife and fork, cup, full canteen, and the day's food ration. The total load could be as much as forty pounds. Veteran troops quickly learned to carry only the essentials in the knapsack or simply roll them in a blanket and tie the blanket over one shoulder. The regiment had received their accoutrements, including their knapsacks, while they were still in Camp Lynnfield but they had to throw them off in the Battle of South Mountain, "never to be seen again." The fact that knapsacks found their way to their owners would seem a small miracle even by today's standards.

got my dress Coat: Inspection of the 150th New York Infantry finds one man wearing his shell jacket–type dress coat; the veteran to his left is in his four-button undress or "sack" coat. A third man, barely visible, is wearing the longer frock-style dress coat.

35th 2: 1863: ". . . and, after a few weeks stay at this place, was sent with the 9th Corps into Kentucky, being stationed at Mount Stirling [Sterling], Lancaster, Stanford, and other places. Lieut. Col. Carruth now became colonel of the regiment."

JQA Journal: (pp. 51–52)

Friday, March 20, 1863: *been snowing all day this Afternoon*

Several different coat/jacket styles can be seen on the men of the 150th New York.

March 21–25, 1863: No Entries

JQA Journal: (p. 53)

Thursday, March 26, 1863: *Struck Tents this morning first thing after breakfast and got ready to start on a pus[h]ing out West*

35th 1: 1863: ". . . thence to Covington, Ky."

Friday, March 27, 1863: *started last night and arrived at Baltimore this morning staid on the boat till near night where we came ashore and took the Cars for Pitts*

Saturday, March 28, 1863: *passed through several small towns passed Harrisburg on the opposite side of the River passed through Altoonia this Evening*

Quincy's Words:

*Cars for Pitts***:** The men boarded Pennsylvania Central Railroad cars to Pittsburgh, Pennsylvania. The overcrowded conditions aboard the "cars" caused the troops to refer to themselves as "Uncle Sam's cattle."

35th 4: March 27–28, 1863: "Landing in Baltimore . . . the brigade marched across the city . . . to the rail-road station. So much had we changed since our first passage through these streets that appearances, which had seemed foreign and almost hostile then, appeared now homelike and friendly; the service had converted us, at least, from provincials to true Union men. Our

The "cars" troops rode were not Pullmans. More often than not they rode in and on cattle, box, and flat cars. Seen here are wounded soldiers being evacuated on open flat-cars where they could easily fall off and where they were exposed to foul weather and exhausting steam from the passing locomotives. Courtesy of the Library of Congress

usual luxurious conveyances—box-cars—were filled with forty men each. Even straw was provided in some. . . . The train did not get fairly started until mid-night; and, when moving, any uncommonly heavy jolt would be followed by a chorus of dashes and exclamation points. In the morning the men found that riding upon the car-tops was as comfortable as within, barring the cinders and tunnels, and certainly better for viewing the scenery, for cattle do not require windows in their cars. Those were merry times, passing through the towns, the boys on top shouting and waving caps and flags, the citizens rushing to doors and windows to respond, small children astonished out of their wits, dogs barking, horses frightened, and a lively time generally. . . . Bound for the great west, what cared we? It was all in the three year's enlistment. At Pittsburg a collation was generously furnished by the citizens, in a hall adorned with flags and mottos. We became sensible to our terrible appearance, when some ladies of the city, being informed that the men were not so rough in manners as in looks, summoned the courage to attend upon us. As we had not seen ourselves in a mirror in six months, a first view was comically surprising—was it possible that the reflections were correct images of the former delicate youths, now browned and smoke stained, hirsute and thread-bare?"

JQA Journal: (pp. 54-55)

Sunday, March 29, 1863: *arrived at Pittsburgh this morning had a splendid bath started for Cincinnati this afternoon mau /// // the cars*

Monday, March 30, 1863: *passed through Columbus The cap-ital of Ohio this morning before night so we will not get a Chance to see the City*

Tuesday, March 31, 1863: *arrived at Cincinnati last night at nrk and had a supper staid in the City till 2 oclock in the morning when we came of on the cars*

Wednesday, April 1, 1863: *started this morning from Coving-ton and after being Delays reached Paris a # distance of from 75 to ur 100 Miles*

35th 1: April 1, 1863: "Moved to Paris [KY]"

Thursday, April 2, 1863: *//to hid our tent this morning near the railrode went up and see Senator Davis's house this Evening and then to meating*

Friday, April 3, 1863: *started this morning and marched all day we are now at mount Sterling*

35th 1: April 3, 1863: "and to Mt. Sterling [KY]."

Quincy's Words:

Senator Davis's house and ***mount Sterling*:** Senator Garrett Davis was born in Mount Sterling, Kentucky. He lived and worked in Bourbon and Montgomery Counties, eventually becoming a lawyer and opening a practice in Paris, Kentucky. He was elected to replace the secessionist John C. Breckinridge in 1861. Breckinridge had just served as vice president of the United States and ran against Lincoln in 1860, but now in 1863, he was a Confederate general and would later be the Confederate Secretary of War.

JQA Journal: (p. 56)

Saturday, April 4, 1863: *Changed our camping ground this morning got a splendid camp now*

Sunday, April 5, 1863: *went to meeting to day and sung in the Chor's*

Monday, April 6, 1863: *been out practicing a little to day the first I have blown since we left Newport News*

Author's Note: March 26–April 6 was an twelve-day hiatus from blowing the bugle for Quincy.

JQA Journal: (pp. 57–59)

April 7–15, 1863: No Entries

35th 4: The regiment receives its "national colors, the stars and stripes. . . . April 8, Major William S. King joined, from home, bringing a fine silk flag . . . sent from Boston by Colonel Wild, and was his last memento to the regiment."

JQA Journal: (p. 60)

Thursday, April 16, 1863: No Entries

Friday, April 17, 1863: *started this morning for Winchester arrived there at 5' o clock after a long and hard march*

Saturday, April 18, 1863: *been exceedingly warm to day every one is searching for a shady place were very tired this morning*

JQA Journal: (p. 61)

Sunday, April 19, 1863: *it̶ much coler than it was yesterday rained a little all the afternoon*

Monday–Tuesday April 20–21, 1863: No Entries

Quincy's Words:

Chor's: or "Choirs"—this would indicate that there was a Sunday Christian religious service for the men in or near camp. Choirs must have been an informal group that sang at these services. Quincy probably had an acceptable singing voice and voluntarily participated. Singing and instrumental music was an extremely important part of the soldiers' life.

went to meeting: Quincy apparently attended church services, or "meetings" on many Sundays.

Winchester: "a pretty village" located about halfway between Mount Sterling and Lexington, Kentucky.

JQA Journal: (pp. 62–63)

April 22–27, 1863: No Entries

JQA Journal: (p. 64)

Tuesday, April 28, 1863: No Entries

Wednesday, April 29, 1863: *been showering all day have had to blow alone to day Gardiner is not well*

Thursday, April 30, 1863: *warm and pleasant. going to be mustered in for pay this after-noon. have been mustered in for pay and were then reviewed by Gen Sturgis*

Quincy's Words:

blow alone: This tells me that normally there were at least two buglers or a small group sounding daily calls with this outfit. This was typical in camps of battalion or regimental size.

Gardiner: He was apparently one of the other buglers with the battalion or regiment. Jason Gardiner of East Weymouth, Massachusetts, is listed as a musician in Company H and served until June 9, 1865.

reviewed by Gen Sturgis: Brigadier General Samuel Davis Sturgis, commander of the Second Division, Ninth Corps, had left it to General Ferrero's Second Brigade to cross the bridge at Antietam Creek and advance up toward the Confederates on the heights west of the bridge and toward Sharpsburg. General Sturgis, a veteran of the Mexican War, had served with the Ninth Corps at the Battles of Wilson's Creek, South Mountain, Antietam, and Fredericksburg. He would go on to serve throughout the war and afterward, assume overall command of the Seventh Cavalry. He would lose a son at the Battle of the Little Big Horn, and have a U.S. Navy transport named after him, as well as a now-famous town in South Dakota.

35th 4: That November at Lenoir Station history records: "The open ground between our color-line and the railroad afforded a good field for evolutions, and morning and afternoon the Thirty-fifth was busy practicing the skirmish drill under the direction of Major Wales. The men soon became proficient in the movements in obedience to the notes of Gardiner's Bugle: 'Forward', 'In retreat', 'Lie down', 'Rise up', 'Commence firing', 'Cease firing', 'Rally', etc."

35th 4: This movement into Kentucky was to "help block the road to any repetation of the operations of the previous autumn [presumably a reference to the threats posed by Confederate General Bragg to East Tennessee which lead to the Battle of Stones River], to assist in covering the railroad communications of Rosecrans . . . to discourage guerillas and prepare for a campaign . . . into East Tennessee. . . ."

35th 4: The troops seemed to find the stops in the various towns along the way interesting and at times enjoyable. These were border areas and the unit's history records: "The people about us were found to be about evenly divided between Union and Confederate sympathies, the same families furnishing members

Brigadier General Samuel Davis Sturgis, commander of the Second Division, Ninth Corps. Courtesy of the Library of Congress

to both causes. . . . The officers of the regiment enjoyed flirtation with the fair Kentucky belles, and many a gilt button was exchanged for a smile from some fair one, who wanted this memento from a hero's breast to pin upon her own. The handsome captain of Company G lost nearly all his buttons in that way." This was probably Captain William Gibson.

JQA Journal: (p. 65)

Friday, May 1, 1863: *warm, and quiet though guard mounting this morning dine well had my picture taken This afternoon going to send it home to morrow*

Saturday, May 2, 1863: *hot and uncomfortable mor drilling to day is saturdays got a letter from Home This afternoon*

Sunday, May 3, 1863: *raining This morning am going to meeting to day if it clears off have been to meeting this Srcrain* [Sunday] *raind hard going down*

Elsewhere in the War: May 1–4, 1863: The Battle of Chancellorsville, Virginia—a tactical Union defeat.

Elsewhere in the War: At Chancellorsville, Confederate General Thomas "Stonewall" Jackson is accidentally shot in his left arm by his own pickets. The removal of his arm weakened him sufficiently to contribute to his death by pneumonia eight days later. The enormity of this to the Confederate cause was forecast by General Lee himself when he said of Jackson, "He has lost his left arm but I have lost my right."

Quincy's Words:

had my picture taken: I believe the photo shown here is the one Quincy had taken in Kentucky. Photography was in its infancy and several technologies had been evolving at the start of the war. The daguerreotype, a silver-coated copper sheet, was giving way to the ambrotype, which was a collodion of nitrated cotton dissolved in ether and alcohol on a glass plate. This technology was better because it did not emit mercury fumes. Both methods were cumbersome and glass plates were delicate. Melainotypes, also called ferrotypes or tintypes, were not fragile and allowed for immediate duplicates

John Quincy Adams; photo believed to have been taken in Kentucky on May 1, 1863. Here he appears to be wearing a standard U.S. Model 1858 forage cap and a shell-style jacket. He has the look of a fit and confident veteran.

on a single plate of tin, but they were a little less sharp than the ambrotype. The tintype made it economically feasible for the common soldier to have his picture taken. Paper-on-card images known as the "carte de visite" (visiting card) or CDV, were a smaller (approximately 2¼ by 4½ inches) form of the albumen print. They were even more inexpensive, easy to mail, and very popular among the soldiers. There are examples of most of these in the "Quincy" collection. This portrait must be a tintype. The photo is fortunately sealed under glass and encased in a brass frame, which in turn is held in a wood, cloth, and leather case. The case is missing its cover panel. I did not attempt to open it for fear of further damage. The collodion appears to be peeling, but was protected from sloughing off by the glass.

JQA Journal: (p. 66)

Monday, May 4, 1863: *started earley this morning and marched 12 miles we are within 7 miles of Lexington hard thunder showers to night*

Tuesday, May 5, 1863: *passed through Lexington this forenoon we are now 8 or 9 miles out of the City are resting now and making coffee camped 6 miles out of Lexington*

Wednesday, May 6, 1863: *passed through Nicholasville this forenoon and camped 9 or 10 miles from the place have marched 45 miles the last 2 days*

35th 1: 1863: *"To Lancaster May 6–7."*

JQA Journal: (p. 67)

Thursday, May 7, 1863: *marched all days passed through Lan-cester to night been going double quick most all day 54th To led off*

Friday, May 8, 1863: *marched till about 1 o clock and went into camp wrote two letters 1 home and one to mary*

Saturday, May 9, 1863: *Splendid morning not going to march to day*

Quincy's Words:

54th led off: This regiment has been chosen to lead the column on this day. At first I wondered if this might refer to the Thirty-Fourth Massachusetts Volunteer Regiment, which is pictured on Page 39, but without a state designation it is difficult to tell. My research was able to show that the Fifty-fourth Mass. was involved in the defense of Washington, D.C. Who then?

mary: Who is Mary? An initial search of Quincy's known relatives did not turn up a Mary. Could this just be a friend from Haverhill or more?

35th 2: 1863: "It was next ordered to Vicksburg, Miss., to reinforce Gen. Grant, remaining about four weeks, until the surrender of the city, July 4."

JQA Journal: (p. 68)

Sunday, May 10, 1863: *started this morning and marched back Lancaster on the same old camping ground we were before*

Monday, May 11, 1863: *had a regimental inspection this afternoon going to be inspected to morrow by an brigade inspector*

Tuesday, May 12, 1863: *been inspected this afternoon*

35th 4: "At Lancaster [KY] the Colonel [Carruth] was, if possible, more exacting than ever; nothing could suit him which was not done on time or at the double-quick. Coming back from Paint Lick special stress was laid upon falling out; the men kept the ranks and files perfectly, and the ten miles were paced off at a rate by the watch, which gave even him satisfaction. Drills were in quick time or double-quick. Shelters were struck, knapsacks packed, lines formed, the regiment countermarched, company streets laid out anew and tents put back up again—all in the space of twenty minutes. In truth, and without exaggeration, the Thirty-Fifth had at this time, under efficient tutelage, become a model regiment in drill, discipline, dress, and arrangement of camp. General Sturgis accompanied by his staff, after viewing one of the parades of the regiments, remarked 'That beats the regulars!'"

JQA Journal: (p. 69)

Wednesday, May 13, 1863: *received two letters one from cbcldy* [?] *and one from Mary*

Thursday, May 14, 1863: *been meeting to day 8 of our drumers have got their discharges*

Friday, May 15, 1863: No Entries

Quincy's Words:

our drumers have got their discharges: I am not sure why this took place. I originally thought that perhaps at this point in the war the buglers were fulfilling

A Union drum corps with the drum major in the foreground. There are also several fifers among the group. Courtesy of the National Archives

the communication needs as previously mentioned and/or the drummers had become "excess baggage" to the future deployment of the regiment or brigade. However, the drum corps is mentioned later in *History of the Thirty-Fifth*, so I remained unclear as to why this took place.

JQA Journal: (pp. 70–71)

May 16–21, 1863: No Entries

Elsewhere in the War: The siege of Vicksburg begins May 19

JQA Journal: (p. 72)

Friday, May 22, 1863: No Entries

Saturday, May 23, 1863: *Started for Crab Orchard arrived within 2 miles of the city this afternoon weather very hot*

35th 1: 1863: ". . . thence to Crab Orchard May 23"

Sunday, May 24, 1863: *no marching today to day tired*

JQA Journal: (p. 73)

Monday, May 25, 1863: *marched through the vilage and camped half a mile from the City*

35th 1: 1863: ". . . and to Stanford May 25."

Tuesday, May 26, 1863: *started last night and marched to Stanford 10 miles sleepy to day*

Wednesday, May 27, 1863: *got our camp laid out and feel rather tired*

35th 4: "On the twenty-third of May the Brigade left Lancaster for Crab Orchard, some twelve miles over very dusty roads . . . stopping over Sunday on the banks of Dick's River . . . where the boys enjoyed a welcome bath. Camp had hardly been laid out . . . at Crab Orchard . . . when an unexpected summons came to proceed at once to Stanford. The distance was only a dozen miles but the cross-road was deep in dust, which rose in suffocating clouds, making the night darker and marching irksome, so that the men reached Stanford in a charming state of ill temper. Camps were passed all along . . . [Finally] we camped on one of those charming lawns, this time almost under the eaves of a mansion house, in which the officers' messes obtained luxurious fare, with even an imp of darkness to keep flies from their elevated noses with a peacock feather brush. The enlisted men, whom the increasing warmth of summer affected with a desire for something lighter than the standard bacon sides and hard bread, sought a change of food. . . . In short it began to be evident that we were waxing fat enough to kill. Taking a sample for Company H: 'Ho, there James!' called the sergeant, 'you are detailed for picket!' 'Picket, sergeant, picket! Why, I ca-a-n't go!' 'Ca-a-n't go; why not?' 'Why, I ca-a-n't go, sergeant, I haven't had my coffee!'"

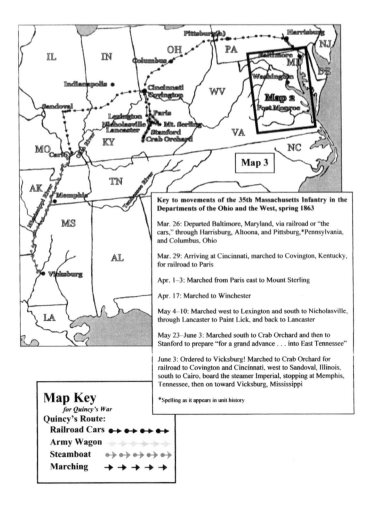

Mid-May 1863: Baton Rouge, Louisiana: Unknown to Quincy at the time, another nineteen-year-old soldier from Haverhill, Massachusetts, Harry Truman Hunkins, who had enlisted as a private for nine months with the

Fiftieth Massachusetts Regiment Volunteer Militia Infantry, died or was killed in action. Harry was a brother to Quincy's future wife. Harry with his regiment had proceeded to White's Bayou "about ten miles southeast from Port Hudson where it [the regiment] remained until the 26th, when it moved up to the works in front of the city [Baton Rouge]. This, like the Vicksburg Campaign, was part of the strategic plan to surround the South and cut it off from the South's trans-Mississippi States. On May 27, the 50th took part in the assault on Port Hudson, its losses however, being slight. It did not participate in the second assault, June 14, but engaged in supporting batteries and in trench duty until the surrender of the city, July 9." ****

JQA Journal: (p. 74)

Thursday, May 28, 1863: *weather warm brigade drill this afternoon*

Friday, May 29, 1863: *warm and sultry been out drilling in the skirmish dril*

Saturday, May 30, 1863: *just received two letters one from ///ine and one from mary massicut// to day*

9th Corps: In June it was ordered to the support of Grant, who was then besieging Vicksburg. Proceeding there promptly, it participated in the investment of that place, although not under fire.

35th 4: When the men learned "where we were bound . . . Vicksburg! Hades Rather! The place, the climate and the warfare thereabouts had at that time the reputation associated with the fiery pit of Gehenna."

JQA Journal: (p. 75)

Sunday, May 31, 1863: *rainy ment to have went to meeting to day if it had not rained*

Monday, June 1, 1863: *been drilling skirmish drill to day no mail*

Tuesday, June 2, 1863: *Warmer and pleasant Gen Ferrero returned to night and has command of the div*

**** William B. Stevens, *History of the Fiftieth Regiment of Infantry, Massachusetts Volunteer Militia, in the Late War of the Rebellion* (Griffith-Stillings Press, 1907).

Quincy's Words:

Mary: Quincy mentions a "Mary" several times in his journal, and the only wartime letter that I am aware of is written to Mary. The only "Mary" I could find in the family genealogy collection was a modern print of a brass-mounted photo of an attractive young woman. Written on the back is: "Robert's mother: Mary Lorenza Parker Adams"...Adams? She appeared in the photo to be about Quincy's age or a few years younger. Had she been his sweetheart? Quincy communicated often to this Mary, but the single existing letter, while showing some bravado, is not a romantic one, nor does he "pine" for her in his journal. However, she was most likely a local girl who had future potential. As it turns out, this *was*

Mary Lorenzo Parker, Quincy's pen pal and future sister-in law

Quincy's Mary, but while he was away, brother Frank must have won her heart. The mystery was finally solved when I rediscovered the envelope that had held the "Bound for Memphis" letter. This Mary had married Frank, Quincy's brother. Her son, Robert Adams, became a well-documented author of folk humor and the family has preserved some of his work, including a set of books entitled *Rude Rural Rhymes*.

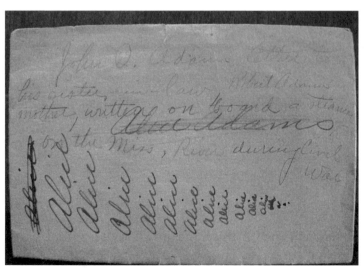

Who was Mary? The mystery was solved when an envelope, thought to be a scrap, revealed the words: "John Q. Adam's letter to his sister-in-law, Robert Adam's mother, written on board a steamer on the Miss. River during Civil War." Quincy's granddaughter, Alice, has used it to write her name many times.

At first I thought the envelope was just a scrap of paper that my aunt Alice, Quincy's number-three granddaughter, had used to practice writing her name multiple times. But as I read the faint penciled words I realized it was true: "Mary" had become Mrs. Frank E. Adams. It would be several years after the war before Quincy would marry another local girl.

This discovery reminded me to photograph or scan everything in the Adams and Hunkins collections, even if I did not know what it was or who the people in it were.

35th 3: June 1863: ". . . joined to the Army of the Tennessee."

JQA Journal: (p. 76)

Wednesday, June 3, 1863: *Rained last night been drilling the battalion as skirmisher's just got and had orders to pack up and start*

35th 1: "Movement to Vicksburg, Miss., June 3–14."

35th 2: 1863: "It was next ordered to Vicksburg, Miss., to reinforce Gen. Grant, remaining about four weeks, until the surrender of the city, July 4."

JQA Journal: (p. 76)

Thursday, June 4, 1863: *marched though the last night and 30 miles begind* (beyond) *1 oclock when we stoped marched to Nickolasvile and took the cars for Covington*

Friday, June 5, 1863: *reached Covington this morning crossed the river into Ohio where we now are waiting for refreshment*

35th 4: "At Nicholasville, while the baggage was being loaded, a locomotive exploded. . . ." This resulted in the death of a soldier of Company C.

Quincy's Words:

marched through the night and thirty miles: This indicates a forced march. The regimental history includes an incident which took place during an all-night march of the "green" troops from Washington toward South Mountain in Maryland. According to *History of the Thirty-Fifth Regiment*, a soldier who had dropped out well along the way into Maryland and had fallen asleep under a wayside hedge, "upon waking . . . came face to face with General Burnside;

making his best salute the man boldly inquired whether the general had seen the thirty-fifth Massachusetts anywhere. 'Oh yes,' replied the urbane general dryly, 'you'll find them all the way from here to Washington!'"

JQA Journal: (p. 77)

Saturday, June 6, 1863: *Rode all night last night and all day to day reached Scandoval at nearly dark changed cars for Cario*

Sunday, June 7, 1863: *reached C this morning been here all day expect to take transport tomorrow*

Monday, June 8, 1863: *Went on board the steamer Imperial to night*

Quincy's Words:

the steamer Imperial: The steamer *Imperial* was a handsome side-wheel river

This woodcut made from a sketch by J. R. Hamilton of the side-wheel steamer *Imperial* docking at New Orleans, appeared in *Harpers Weekly* magazine, August 8, 1863. It was reportedly the first steamer to make the passage from St. Louis after the Union victories at Vicksburg and Baton Rouge in July of 1863. Illustration courtesy of harpersweekly.com.

passenger transport boat. When I was doing research on Mississippi River system steamboats, the first picture to appear was a woodcut of the *Imperial* from an 1863 *Harper's Weekly*. The *Imperial* is reported to be the first Union boat to traverse the Mississippi after it was opened up by the fall of Vicksburg, Baton Rouge, and other Confederate strongholds.

JQA Journal: (p. 78)

Tuesday, June 9, 1863: *Got aground on a sand bar and laid still all night got off early this morning*

Author's Note: Quincy writes the "Bound for Memphis" letter, probably while they were grounded on the sandbar. Both the actual letter and a typewritten transcript were discovered in the family archives.

Wednesday, June 10, 1863: *been going all day reached Memphis at 5 PM stad here all night get paid off*

Thursday, June 11, 1863: *Been in M all day had a bully time*

Quincy's Words:

Been in M all day had a bully time: Quincy at nineteen years was a healthy American boy out on the town. Memphis during the Civil War had a reputation for being able to show young men a good time.

For many years we believed that the "Bound for Memphis" letter was written on June 9, 1862. It turns out that when my mother had typed the transcription in the early 1950s, she understandably mistook Quincy's 3 for a

On board the Steamer
Imperial on the Miss. Rv.

Bound for Memphis June 9th, '62

Dear Mary

I am right on my travel lately, came on board last night at Cairo, are now 50 or 60 miles from that place. We touched the shore on the Missouri side a few minutes ago. I went ashore so I can say I have been in Mo. I have been in 14 different states in the Union, quite a traveler. The battery have got their guns in position as there is such a thing as our being fired upon and of course we should be impolite if we did not return the compliment. We are going to be paid off this afternoon, 2 months of pay. Passed Island No. 10 about 3 hours ago. There is nothing particularly interesting about the place now. There are any quantity of wrecks along the shore. It is raining quite hard now. You and I will just have to take a turn down this way after the war is over and see the country. Are having a gay time now, plenty of room and everything is lovely. We had a mail last night but I didn't get anything, don't see the meaning of it. There must be some mistake about it, probably shall not get another till we get to Vicksburg, may get one at Memphis. The band are on board with us, the band that came out with the 11th. It is the finest band in the Army. I am going to send 15 dollars home by Adams Esq. Co. from Memphis. There is a good pianoforte on board but none are allowed to go into the cabin but the officers; should like to get a chance to play on it a little. I reckon we will get V, and come home this fall. Rains pretty hard now. We shall get wet in spite of all we can do, shall have to lay in the wet, but it won't hurt us any. Should have been glad of this place when we were on picket at Fredericksburg. I will see the mail is going at 2 o'clock this afternoon. Will send this first chance.

Yours as ever,

John Q. Adams
Haverhill, Mass.

Typewritten transcription of the Bound for Memphis letter found in the Adams family archives

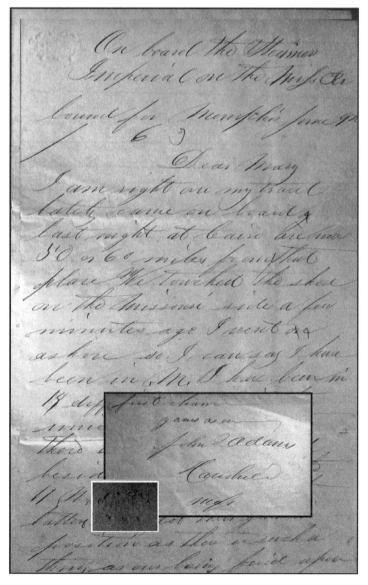

A collage of the first page of the actual "Bound for Memphis" letter with a close-up of the greeting area and an enhancement of the paper's watermark. Quincy has used his Haverhill address even though he was on the Mississippi River when the letter was written.

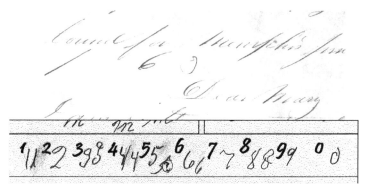

Pictured is an enlargement of the date and greeting area of the actual letter above the numeral portion of the author's decoder sheet, for comparison of Quincy's 2's and the 3's.

2. According to the *Regimental History*, the unit was not formed until July and August of 1862 and departed Massachusetts in August 1862. The mystery was solved by comparing Quincy's written 2's and 3's using the Quincy Handwriting Chart. The numeral following the Quincy "6" is much more like the chart "3" than the "2," and his journal puts him on the *Imperial* on June 9, **1863**.

35th 4: "In the morning of June 7 we were at the jumping-off point—Cairo—disembarking from the cars upon the levee. . . . The immense steamboat Imperial, with decks tier above tier, was assigned to carry General Ferrero and staff, the Eleventh New Hampshire, Benjamin's Battery 'E' Section U.S. Artillery and our regiment . . . and swung with the current out of the Ohio upon the broad Mississippi, whose winding course we were to follow for some five hundred miles.

"The name of places . . . served as mile-posts to mark our descent: Columbus, with General Polk's old fortifications, where we ran aground and stuck all night; Belmont, opposite, where General Grant made his first essay in the war; Island 10, which we passed on the ninth, the scene of General Pope's victory; Memphis, reached on the tenth, famous for its gun-boat fight; Helena, where we hitched up to the bank on the twelfth, which was, within a few weeks after our visit, to be attacked and bravely defended; Milliken's Bend, on the thirteenth . . . and Arkansas on the west, Kentucky and Tennessee on the east, and now, as we approached our goal, Louisiana on the west and Mississippi on the east."

JQA Journal: (p. 79)

Friday, June 12, 1863: *started early this morning and have been going all day*

Saturday, June 13, 1863: *Have had 3 Gun bouts with us ever since we left M expect to be attacked*

Sunday, June 14, 1863: *landed this morn-ing in full view of V the mortar bout are shelling the city constantly*

35th 1: *June 14–July 4, 1863:* The regiment become involved in the Siege of Vicksburg.

Quincy's Words:

in full view of V the mortar bout(s) are shelling the city constantly: Mortar boats were armored wooden vessels armed with mortars.

This view graphically portrays the fury of the Union fleet's mortar attack on the key Confederate city of Vicksburg, Mississippi. Its fall would cut off and complete the surrounding of the Confederate states east of the Mississippi River. Unarmed transport vessels can be seen passing protected behind the armored gunboats. Courtesy of the Library of Congress

JQA Journal: (p. 80)

Monday, June 15, 1863: *marched across the point of land to the mrks below expecting to cross the river to waringtn didnt but marched back*

Tuesday, June 16, 1863: *Took the bout Omaha and went up the Yazzo river to Haines bluff staid on the bout all night*

Wednesday, June 17, 1863: *landed and marched to mill dale 3 (o)r 4 miles from, H.B.* [Haines Bluff, MS]

JQA Journal: (p. 81)

June 18–20, 1863: No Entries

9th Corps: The "Vicksburg campaign [May 19–July 4 1863] had not cost the corps the bloody tribute exacted in previous campaigns, still it was no less destructive of life, as disease made fearful inroads in the ranks. Among those who succumbed to the deadly malaria of the Vicksburg camps, was General Welsh, who, soon after, went home to die."

A mortar bombardment was an awesome and terrifying event. Mortars were very short cannons made specifically to lob projectiles over fortification walls in a high-arcing trajectory. The mortar usually launched bombs, called shells, which were hollow cast iron balls filled with gunpowder and plugged with a fuse. The fuse could be adjusted just prior to firing, to be timed to explode at a certain

The projectile on the left is an intact eight-inch mortar shell that is documented as having been found in the outskirts of Vicksburg. The loading/fuse hole is plugged with a new wooden plug. The lifting notches can be clearly seen. The six-inch wood decking provides a scale. The shell fragment of an exploded eleven-inch shell shows the thickness and the loading/fuse hole in cross-section. This example would have taken a screw-in–type metal timing fuse. The wooden timing fuse shown atop the fragment is an actual Civil War–era fuse. The hole visible on the end would have been filled with powder then covered with a paper seal. It is marked off in tenths of an inch and would have been cut off on the small end to the proper timing line. The loaded and timed fuse would then be jammed into the hole just before firing. The explosion of the propelling charge would ignite the fuse. **Artifacts courtesy of Kevin Umhey Collection**

distance or height above the target, showering the shattered case fragments or sometimes musket balls downward at great velocity.

JQA Journal: (p. 82)

June 21–22, 1863: No Entries

Tuesday, June 23, 1863: *broke camp to night and marched hard towards the landing raining*

35th 4: *June 15–29, 1863*: After initially putting ashore at Sherman's Landing on the Louisiana side, it was decided not to place the division, by way of the swamp, at the south end of the city, which was believed to be the weakest defensibly. "The regiment went aboard . . . the Omaha and . . . paddled up the Yazoo to Haines's Bluff . . ." then marched to Milldale, Mississippi. The Confederates had pulled back toward Vicksburg and one morning ". . . a heavy explosion . . . and heavier firing than usual was heard from the direction of the city. Upon another morning General Grant visited our encampment and called on General Parke who commanded our Corps. . . . On the twenty-ninth we moved . . . to Oak Ridge . . . Here we relieved some of Sherman's men, tall and straight fellows, with their impressive felt hats, some had Henry repeating rifles. They were full of stories about the fights at Champion's Hills and other places and we listened with interest. To be sure the losses at Fredericksburg alone in one day had been many more than their whole campaign, but Eastern soldiers were not inclined to boast of that day, and the Western vim and self-confidence were so different from the tone of the Eastern army it was a pleasure to listen to their talk. We accepted in silence the epithets of Holiday Soldiers . . . trusting to the course of events, rather than our tongues, to prove our mettle."

This dramatic view of the Union Mississippi River Fleet provides a look at the type of stern wheel transport vessel typical on western rivers. Anchored nearby is a U.S Navy ironclad gunboat used to escort the troops in hostile waters. This view is near Cairo, Illinois, at the confluence of the Ohio and Mississippi Rivers. Quincy passed through this junction twice during General Grant's successful campaign to surround and isolate the Confederate states east of the river. This essentially completed the blockade of the South and brought to fruition the goal of General Winfield Scott's original Anaconda Plan. The U.S. Navy played a hugely important role in winning the war. Courtesy of the U.S. Army Heritage and Education Center, the MOLLUS-MASS Civil War Photograph Collection

JQA Journal: (p. 83)

Wednesday, June 24, 1863: *been busy to day pulling trees and digging riffle pit*

Thursday, June 25, 1863: *nothing mor new still at mortar intrenchment*

Friday, June 26, 1863: No Entries

Quincy's Words:

pulling trees and digging riffle pit: In preparing a defensive site, trees would be cut around a spot on higher ground to clear the field of view and deprive the enemy of protective cover. The leafy brush would be removed or burned, and the limbs with branches sharpened and placed pointing out would form abatis. This would entangle advancing skirmishers and discourage or break up an enemy charge. (See page 132, lower image.) Pits would be dug around or across the site to be defended, usually on higher ground, with the excavated soil thrown up around the circumference to provide cover for riflemen.

mortar intrenchment: As mentioned before, mortars were essentially bomb-launching cannons meant to be fired in a high-arcing trajectory over and into the defenses of the enemy. They were generally larger and much more cumbersome than field artillery. When set up in a semi permanent location they would be placed in deep entrenchments. Large mortars were more typically used in the siege of forts and cities such as Vicksburg. A howitzer was halfway between a mortar and a field gun. Howitzers were more mobile and therefore, like field guns, more quickly deployed.

This lantern-slide image shows huge thirteen-inch mortars in their entrenchment. Larger cannons such as these were difficult to transport and were usually carried by railroad or aboard boats. They were used primarily in siege work. At the siege of Vicksburg, Quincy wrote in his journal as being in full view of the mortar bombardment. Courtesy of the Library of Congress

35th 4: *Mid-June, 1863:* "Where we were it was only necessary to throw up breastworks upon the ridge selected, cut down the trees, which grew quickly upon the outer side, for a slashing or abatis; plant the artillery at commanding angles, and a line was established which was impregnable. General Johnston knew the difficulties of the approach and kept a respectful distance, near Bird-song's Ferry, inclining rather to the south, down the Big Black—which ran across our front. . . . As soon as the work of digging this line was commenced, we moved a mile near the Yazoo River landing, and pitched tents upon a side hill, in order to be near the scene of our labor."

JQA Journal: (pp. 84–85)

June 27–30, 1863: No Entries

July 1–2, 1863: No Entries

Elsewhere in the War: The Battle of Gettysburg begins July 1, 1863. This battle has been referred to as the "high watermark of the Confederacy."

July 2, 1863: "THE DAILY CITIZEN, the last operating newspaper in besieged Vicksburg, Mississippi lies in its carriage ready for its last article. The Confederates were all out of news print paper and rolls of wall paper were substituted. The Daily Citizen's printers never returned."

The Daily Citizen of Vicksburg dated July 2, 1863, as photographed through its broken glass frame, as well as the banner and first two paragraphs containing a mix of news, morale building, humor, and propaganda

The text of the banner and the first two paragraphs provide the reader with an interesting view of the Confederate perspective of the siege.

THE DAILY CITIZEN

J. M Swords, ... Proprietor

Vicksburg, Miss.

THURSDAY, JULY 2, 1863.

Mrs. Cisco was instantly killed on Monday, on Jackson road. Mrs. Cisco's husband is now in Virginia, a member of Moody's artillery, and the death of such a winning, affectionate and dutiful wife will be a loss to him irreparable.

We are indebted to Major Gillespie for a steak of Confederate beef *alias* meat. We have tried it, and can assure our friends that if it is rendered necessary, they need have no scruples at eating the meat. It is sweet, savory and tender, and so long as we have a mule left we are satisfied our soldiers will be content to subsist on it.

JQA Journal: (p. 86)

Friday, July 3, 1863: No Entries

Saturday, July 4, 1863: *Vicksburg surrendered this morning at 5 o clock got orders to be ready to move immediately got a mail The first we have had*

Elsewhere in the War: General Lee's army withdraws from Gettysburg, the "high-water mark" of the Confederacy. Lee's invasion of the North fails and his army turns south.

35th 4: "On the fourth of July . . . cannonading toward the city had ceased."

Elsewhere in the War: One hundred and seventeen miles south and down-river, Private Harry Truman Hunkins, of the Fiftieth Massachusetts Volunteer Militia Regiment, dies during the siege of Port Hudson, Louisiana. Harry was the brother of Quincy's future wife.

Sunday, July 5, 1863: *Marched a little while last night and halted in a corn field been marching all day today*

35th 1: July 5–10, 1863: Advance on Jackson, Miss.

July 4, 1863: Vicksburg surrenders to the Union siege and the office of *The Daily Citizen* falls into Union hands. In the small remaining space below the last two articles of Confederate propaganda is a note placed by Union occupiers.

The following two paragraphs are transcriptions of Confederate morale-boosting propaganda aimed at keeping spirits high within the besieged city.

The last three paragraphs of *The Daily Citizen*. The upper two are a continuation of the Confederate text, and the last and somewhat bolder text was added by the Yankees after the surrender of the city. A transcription is provided.

The third is of the last paragraph, which appeared in bold, added by the conquering Yankees.

The Yanks outside our city are considerably on the sick list. Fever, dysentery and disgust are their companions, and Grant is their master. The boys are deserting daily and are crossing the river in the region of Warrenton, cursing Grant and abolitionists generally. The boys are down upon the earth delving, the burrowing, the bad water and the hot weather.

GONE OUT. – The National Intelligencer of Washington, has closed its long career in a suspension and sale of its effects at auction. It has been highly respectable and mischievous in its day and generation. An old Union prop falls with it. If we had the writing of its epitaph we should say, "Old Grimes is dead."

NOTE.

JULY 4th, 1863.

Two days bring about great changes. The banner of the Union floats over Vicksburg. Gen. Grant has "caught the rabbit;" and has dined in Vicksburg, and he did bring his dinner with him. The "Citizen" lives to see it. For the last time it appears on "Wall paper." No more will it imagine the luxury of mule meat and fricassed kitten—urge Southern warriors to such diet never more. This is the last wall paper edition, and is, excepting this note, from the types as we found them. It will be valuable hereafter as a curiosity.

)((

At first I wondered if this had been retrieved by Quincy and brought home as a trophy, but I had left that thought for future consideration. Quincy would have been totally unaware of this interesting curiosity and would not have had the opportunity to collect one as they were on the march the night of July 4. We believe that the "Quincy" specimen would never have survived his odyssey still to come. However, this specimen was in good condition and had been carefully mounted and encased in glass. By the time I had photographed it through the glass, the rear pain of glass had accidentally broken from a fall off the wall and its elderly caretaker had not had an opportunity to get it repaired. More recently the relic came under the care of the youngest of the cousins and the second son of the youngest of the Adams daughters, my aunt Barbara. Cousin Pete sought to have it remounted before I could photograph it sans glass.

During the process, Pete had become suspicious of its origin. It had been in the family since any living memory could recall and it was, after all, quite venerable looking and obviously old. Pete had discovered a website that discussed common fake historic newspapers and the *Vicksburg Daily Citizen* was there right at the head of the list. It discussed the original newspaper and then the existence of several known "fakes." Apparently several different common reproductions were made as souvenirs during the 1870s and '80s for sale at G.A.R. reunions and celebrations with no intention of deceit. The author of the website provided several very helpful diagnostic tools to make it easy to spot the "fakes." Several of these reprints were marked as such but several were not. Some of these were on period wallpaper but not matching the original patterns. Others were not done with the exact same layout, errors, and text. Almost immediately Pete saw that in column one, line two of Quincy's edition, there were more than six periods between the proprietor's name and "Proprietor": J.M. Sword,......Proprietor. Ours has eighteen. This was the first of several clues listed and made it possible for Pete to be able to ascertain that this was *not* an original, but it was an early reproduction and probably a G.A.R.-associated souvenir. This and similar websites are invaluable for new collectors of Civil War artifacts to protect themselves from unscrupulous or unwitting sellers. They also allow the non-expert researcher to do a project such as this.

Harry Truman Hunkins (mentioned earlier) of the Fiftieth Massachusetts Volunteer (infantry) Militia, a nine-month unit, died or was killed on July 3, 1863, at Baton Rouge, Louisiana. He was buried the same day and is now

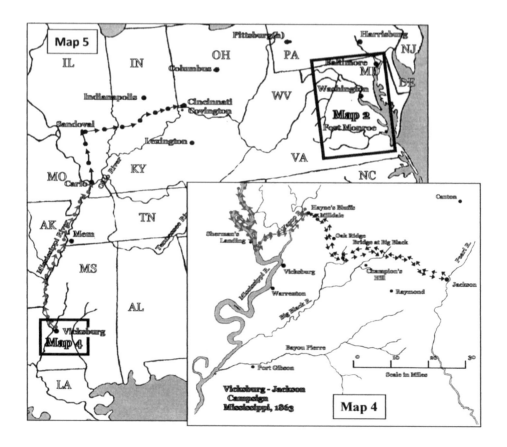

interned in the Baton Rouge National Cemetery. An account from the Massachusetts Civil War Research Center describes the months leading up to the surrender of Baton Rouge: "On May 12 [1863] the [Fiftieth Mass.] regiment proceeded to White's Bayou [La.] about ten miles southeast from Port Hudson where it remained until the 26th when it moved up to the works in front of the City. It took part in the assault on Port Hudson, May 27, its losses, however, being slight. It did not participate in the second assault, June 14, but was engaged in supporting batteries and in trench duty until the surrender of the city, July 9."*****

A document discovered among miscellaneous family genealogical files and a photo among the Hunkins material were all that remained of this young man's life. The document indicated that his last five months' pay was claimed by his older brother on behalf of their father, over a year after his death. It reads:

***** "History of the Fiftieth Regiment Massachusetts Volunteer Militia Infantry, Nine Months," The Massachusetts Civil War Research Center.

"Sir: Enclosed you will receive a certificate No. 116029 for $53.30 payable to you as father of the deceased or to your order, by any Paymaster of the U.S. Army, being pay due Harry T. Hunkins of late, Private in Captain Duncan's Company F, 50 Regiment of Mas. Vols. For services from the 28 day of February 1863, when last paid to the 3 day of July 1863, time of his death ~~and the $100 Bounty allowed by Act July, 22,1861~~, Nine month men are not entittled to the Bounty.

Very respectfully, Your obedient servant, E. B. Linch, Second Auditor, [and signed by his older brother Ensign Lewis Hunkins.

Receipt for final pay of the deceased soldier, Harry T. Hunkins

Old documents such as this are invaluauable to the researcher, and even the amateur. While working on the history of Ashokan for use in our interpretive program, I found myself delving through copies of old deeds and maps in the County Clerk's Hall of Records. One of the peculiarities I often came across was an unfamiliar letter; I mistakenly took it for an "f". It turned out to be an "ſ". You will notice one in the document above in the abbreviation of the state: Maſs. This letter is one of the last vestiges of the old English alphabet, which also had several other letters and ligatures. It represents the long "s" sound, and is often found in the doubled "s" situation in handwritten documents up until the mid-1800s.

This ambrotype found with Ensign Lewis Hunkins's Civil War material is most certainly Harry Truman Hunkins.

9th Corps: "Upon the surrender of Vicksburg, Parke's two divisions joined the main army in its movement on Jackson, and became engaged in the fighting there, with a loss of 34 killed, 229 wounded, and 28 missing; total, 291."

JQA Journal: (p. 87)

Monday, July 6, 1863: *Marched till late last night had a very hard shower*

July 7–8, 1863: No Entries

35th 4: GENERAL ORDER, No. 52 "Headquarters of the Expedition," Camp at Flox, July 6, 1863.

> *"IV.—The movement [of this division] will begin at four o'clock P.M. of July 6 (today) VI.—All commanders will hold their troops in perfect order of battle at all times, and on encountering the enemy will engage him at once. VII. – Private pillage and plunder must cease; our supplies are now ample; . . . . . the people of the country should be protected as far as possible against wanton acts of irresponsible parties, etc. 'By order of Maj. Gen. SHERMAN, R. M. Sawyer, A. A. G. Official: G. H. McKibben, A. A .G.'"*

35th 2: 1863: The division participated in the pursuit of Johnston's army to Jackson, Mississippi.

35th 1: July 10–17, 1863: Siege of Jackson

JQA Journal: (p. 88)

Thursday, July 9, 1863: *Got any quantity of meal and molasses This afternoon after getting all the provision we could cary we burned the house*

Friday, July 10, 1863: *have not marched far to day as we are near Jackson*

Saturday, July 11, 1863: *Our boys cleaned out th a house this morning I went and played a piano Forte that was there*

Quincy's Words:

meal and molasses: Meal would have been cornmeal for bread making, and molasses is a by-product of the processing of (in this case, most likely) sugar beets, a common crop in the eastern central states at that time.

after getting all the provision we could cary we burned the house and ***Our boys cleaned out a house this morning***: Clearly these journal lines indicate that heavy foraging was taking place. It was next to impossible to provision and feed, by way of normal channels, a many thousand–man army marching rapidly over captured territory. Foraging was virtually the only way to supplement the meager rations the men were able to carry. Armies commonly needed to enhance their food rations for men and horses and did so by collecting any livestock or crops that were handy to their movements. Large armies in the Civil War could devastate a wide swath along their route as they scoured the land for anything edible. It also appeared that a scorched-earth policy was being undertaken, a tactic that General Sherman would use to inflict a mortal wound on the Confederacy the following year. The war was now being waged against the ability and will of the civilian population to support their army and cause. Apparently "General Order 52" had not reached the Thirty-Fifth yet.

piano Forte: is the old name for what today we would just call a piano. Interestingly, in musical terms, the term "piano" means "soft" and "forte" means "loud," referring to the wide variation in the volume attainable by the instrument.

JQA Journal: (p. 89)

Sunday, July 12, 1863: *came down by the Asylum yesterday been supporting the skirmishers today and under fire all the time*

Monday, July 13, 1863: *had 6 man abandoned yesterday the 14th Rode-island regt. relieved us this morning had 9 men killed the first thing*

Tuesday, July 14, 1863: *got relieved this morning for a couple days The boys are very tired and need ~~rest~~ rest rest*

Quincy's Words:

the Asylum: This was a facility for the mentally ill, or in the words of the regimental history, it was "the State Asylum for the Insane."

6 man abandoned: This probably means that these men were wounded while skirmishing or lost in the dark and could not get back to the line before being taken prisoner.

14th Rode Island: My research found that the Fourteenth Rhode Island was a heavy artillery regiment formed in the summer of 1863. It was Rhode Island's first black Civil War regiment. That unit's history places it in the coastal defense of Narragansett Bay in the fall of 1863 and in early 1864 on the coast of Texas, and then to the defenses of New Orleans and Baton Rouge. This left me with a mystery as to the unit that Quincy had caught up with. The Fourteenth New Hampshire was in the Second Brigade, Second Division, Ninth Army Corps, Army of the Tennessee[******] in July of 1863 and in the Vicksburg Campaign, as was the Thirty-Fifth. More likely, this was the Seventh Rhode Island, which had been transferred to the Ninth Corps at the end of September 1862. The regimental history would later confirm this. After further enhancement of that portion of the journal I could see that what I had originally took to be a faint fourteen was actually the quickly formed seven of an exhausted soldier.

35th 4: "The men lay low or kept behind trees, exchanging shots with their opponents—who lurked undercover the same way—and watched the artillery duel. Lieutenant Benjamin, with his favorite twenty-pounders, opened on the

---

[******]   The Army of the Tennessee was the Union army designation in the Western Theater of War, as opposed to Lee's Army of Tennessee

enemy; once or twice, while getting the range, dropping a shell short into our line, in that pleasant way the gunners had of letting the infantry know they had artillery support. The Confederates who manned the cotton battery were the noisiest lot we ever listened to; we were so close as to easily hear everything, their words of command, the discharges, and the yells which they gave every time, with the compliments they sent with the shot. The noise they made seemed to keep up their courage, and as for their missiles they went whirring overhead in search of the lunatics in the Asylum."

35th 4: "At night the men were ordered to fix bayonets and receive any sallying party with cold steel. The only event was the missing of our lines by the men returning from the rear in the darkness; Sergeant Luther S. Bailey, of Company G, in this way wandered over to the Confederates and was taken prisoner."

35th 4: "At daylight, July 13, we were, in turn, relieved by the seventh Rhode Island. In coming forward for that purpose, they made what seemed to us rather too much racket with orders and tin pots rattling upon bayonets. The enemy thought it an advance of our lines, and commenced shooting in a brisk manner at once, keeping up a more steady firing all day, to the damage of the Seventh, who lost some fifteen killed and wounded. As they started the game we were content to let them play it out, and retired into the reserve line to cook the longed for coffee."

35th 4: July 13, **1863:** "The enemy continued very uneasy all day; the Thirty-Fifth lay in support as upon the first day. . . . At one time during the day the efforts of the enemy were so violent as to appear like an attempt to break our front line; the humming of the bullets was quite lively, and the regiment formed, moved into position, and even charged forward a little way; but finally, the Confederates desisted and the line quieted down."

JQA Journal: (p. 90)

Wednesday, July 15, 1863: *Nothing new to day expect to have to go on duty again to morrow*

Thursday, July 16, 1863: *Started early this morning and went up to the front are supporting the skirmishers to day expect to be skirmishing to morrow ourselves*

Friday, July 17, 1863: *The rebs evacuated jackson last night our regt was the first in the city this morning any quantity of vinegar or molasses*

35th 2: 1863: "... and [the regiment] was present at the capture of the city ..."

The battle-tested and tattered Stars and Stripes placed on the Missouri State Capitol building July 17, 1863, by the Thirty-Fifth Massachusetts. Courtesy of the Massachusetts Art Commission

35th 4: The Northern newspapers mistakenly gave the "first" honors to the Thirty-Fifth Missouri, probably thinking that it was not possible for a Massachusetts regiment to have been there.

Quincy's Words:

Skirmishers: An army on the move protected itself with lines of skirmishers. These were troops deployed in loose formation ahead of, or on the flanks of, the main body of soldiers. These troops drew the enemy's fire, thus alerting the main body to the location of the enemy position.

Skirmishers of the 150th New York confront Confederate skirmishers on the hill above at the Ashokan Civil War Days.

JQA Journal: (p. 91)

Saturday, July 18, 1863: *Everything is quiet it is thought by some that we are going back to /y hap/ we are*

Sunday, July 19, 1863: *got orders to be ready to march at 4 o clock to night dont think we shall go till to morrow*

Monday, July 20, 1863: *Started from Jackson early this morning marched 20 miles to day very hot*

35th 2: 1863: ". . . then returned to its old camp near Vicksburg."

JQA Journal: (p. 92)

Tuesday, July 21, 1863: *marched early this morning 20 miles any quantity of men sun struck camped in a cornfield to night*

Wednesday, July 22, 1863: *Moved from the cornfield into woods and staid till 4 P.M. when we started once more had a big shower to night marched 10 or 12 miles*

Thursday, July 23, 1863: *Started early this morning and marched 8 or 10 miles and reached our old camp at Mill Dale pretty well played out*

JQA Journal: (p. 93)

July 24–26, 1863: No Entries

35th 1: 1863: "At Milldale until August 6."

35th 4: 1863: "Some stragglers were stopped by guerillas and lost their watches, but were themselves released. The rest came along in squads, and a ragged, mud-bespattered lot they were, but right glad to ground arms at the spring and quench a thirst made insatiable by past deprivation."

JQA Journal: (p. 94)

July 27–29, 1863: No Entries

JQA Journal: (p. 95)

Thursday, July 30, 1863: No Entries

Friday, July 31, 1863: *Went out this morning about 5 miles*

Saturday, August 1, 1863: *Were relieved this morning and came back to camp Musquitoes very thick last night*

Quincy's Words:

***Musquitoes very thick*:** This is low country with a high water table. Stagnant water collected in the myriad of depressions and combined with a warm, moist climate formed an ideal environment for mosquitoes and their larvae to survive and flourish in huge numbers. In the days before pest-mitigating practices, insect netting, and repellant, it created not only almost unbearable living conditions but a dangerous health situation.

JQA Journal: (p. 96)

August 2–4, 1863: No Entries

35th 3: 1863: "August . . . returned to service the Department of the Ohio."

JQA Journal: (p. 97)

Wednesday, August 5, 1863: *Have been quite sick not eaten much*

Thursday, August 6, 1863: *Broke camp this afternoon and marched down to the landing was just played out got 1 hif*

Modes of travel: Both Quincy and the regimental history refer to the "cars," meaning railroad cars. The "wagons" are covered army wagons as seen here. Courtesy of the Library of Congress

35th 1: August 6–14, 1863: "Moved to Cincinnati, Ohio . . ."

On August 6, 1863, the Thirty-Fifth moved north on a river "bout" to Cairo, Illinois, and boarded the railroad "cars" to Cincinnati, Ohio. The regiment crossed the river [presumably the Ohio River] and marched to Hickman's Bridge to catch the "wagons" on August 18.

35th 2: 1863: "From here it [the Thirty-Fifth] proceeded by bout and train to Cincinnati. . . . ."

Author's Note: The sentence above is one of several occurrences in the various histories and Quincy's writing where the spelling of "boat" is "bout." This particular "bout" was the steamboat Planet.

Friday, August 7, 1863: *Started last night rode all night and all day to day have been quite sick*

Quincy's Words:

quite sick: Quincy probably contracted a dose of malaria. While malaria is primarily a tropical and subtropical disease, it does occur in the damp portions of warmer states such as Mississippi and, while it can be very serious, is surviv-able. It is caused by a protozoan parasite carried by mosquitoes and injected during the bite of the female. Its symptoms include high fevers, shaking chills, and anemia. Following his mosquito-infested camp experience, he records about a week of sickness, including the shakes. An excerpt from the regimental history provides a glimpse of the climate, and the physical and psychological state of the men.

35th 4: "Those days at Milldale were too warm for any but the most moder-ate exertion; about four in the afternoon, there would be a shower of more or less violence, everything remaining wet and steaming until morning. The deep trench we had dug for a rifle-pit on the summit of our hill had collected such a body of water that finally it burst forth, came rushing down the steep, and swept away several tents, scattering the contents all abroad, to the no small discomfort of the inmates and amusement of their comrades. Many of the regiment were ill, prostrated by the climate, but those who retained health enjoyed themselves in a quiet way." At Milldale the regiment lost four men to malaria and three more on the passage upriver.

35th 4: "On the sixth of August the regiment marched down to Haines's Bluff and on board the steamboat Planet, which was already crowded . . . progress up the river was similar to the journey down but slower, and the depth was less, requiring careful pilotage. The Planet was very much inferior to the old Imperial, and our quarters were uncomfortably crowded. When all the deck space, outside and in, was occupied there was hardly room for each man to lie down, and when a man had appropriated his six feet of plank, by depositing his pack or spreading his shelter tent over it, he kept it all the way rain or shine."

JQA Journal: (p. 98)

Saturday, August 8, 1863: *Arrived at Memphis this afternoon am so sick that I cant go ashore*

Sunday, August 9, 1863: *Started from Memphis this afternoon weather is very hot*

Monday, August 10, 1863: *Weather continues hot had the shakes last night*

JQA Journal: (p. 99)

Tuesday, August 11, 1863: *nothing new had the shakes again last night*

Wednesday, August 12, 1863: *reached Cairo this morning at sunrise am feeling better left Cairo the cars this afternoon*

Thursday, August 13, 1863: *arrived at Sandoval this morning and changed cars for Cincinnati*

Quincy's Words:

left Cairo [on] the cars: In 1863 the Illinois Central Railroad ran due north out of Cairo, about 113 railroad miles to Sandoval. Cairo is at the southern apex of Illinois on the confluence of the Mississippi and Ohio Rivers.

changed cars for Cincinnati: Sandoval was the junction with the Ohio and Mississippi Railroad, which ran east and west, from St. Louis, Missouri, to Cincinnati, Ohio.

9th Corps: "The corps left Mississippi in August 1863 and returned to Kentucky, where, after a short rest, it joined in Burnside's advance into East Tennessee, a movement that had already been commenced. The two divisions were now reduced to about six thousand men. General Parke was chief of staff of the Army of the Ohio, General Robert B. Potter succeeded to the command of the corps, and Generals Hartranft and Ferrero were in command of the two divisions."

JQA Journal: (p. 100)

Friday, August 14, 1863: *arrived at Cincinnati this afternoon had a good supper and crossed the river into Ky*

35th 2: 1863: "... **reaching there** [Cincinnati] **the 14th of August.**"

Saturday, August 15, 1863: *Laid out our camp ground this morning and pitched our tents*

Sunday, August 16, 1863: *Weather is not as hot as in Mh'ps nothing in particular to do*

JQA Journal: (p. 101)

Monday, August 17, 1863: *The other regts have been paid off it is reported that we are to go to Hickman bridge t gain a wagon train*

35th 1: 1863: *"At Covington, Ky., until August 18. Marched to Nicholasville August 18–25."*

Tuesday, August 18, 1863: *beat reveille this morning at 8 o clock expect to march today marched to day all day cught the wagons to night*

Wednesday, August 19, 1863: *Started this morning at half past 6 rode on the wagons camp at Crittenden to night*

Quincy's Words:

beat reveille: This is evidence that Quincy was also, on occasion at least, a drummer.

wagons *and* ***wagon train:*** It appears that the regiment or some of its members were able to ride on the wagons for up to several days. These wagons were typically hauled by mules.

JQA Journal: (p. 102)

Thursday, August 20, 1863: *Rode about 23 miles to day*

Friday, August 21, 1863: *Camped near Georgetown to night*

Saturday, August 22, 1863: *Passed through Georgetown this morning camped at Paris to night*

JQA Journal: (p. 103)

Sunday, August 23, 1863: *been in Paris all day start for Lexington to morrow morning*

Monday, August 24, 1863: *Start this morning passed through Lexington about noon had a hard thunder shower to night*

A wagon train, identified as that of the Second Vermont Regiment early in the war, is seen approaching Camp Griffin. The tents have already been unloaded and wagons are undoubtedly bringing up the remainder of the heavy gear and provisions. Courtesy of the Library of Congress

Tuesday, August 25, 1863: *passed through nicholasville this afternoon camped about 8 miles from n.*

JQA Journal: (p. 104)

Wednesday, August 26, 1863: *Expect to camp here for a short time*

Thursday, August 27, 1863: *Had a mail to day the first we have had since we left Lexington got 3 letters*

Friday, August 28, 1863: *Got another mail to day reced one letter from home*

JQA Journal: (pp. 105–107)

August 29–September 6, 1863: No Entries

N.G. Map: "This City [Knoxville, TN], which remained loyal to the Union, remained in Confederate hands until September 2, 1863, when it yielded to Burnside's advance."

JQA Journal: (p. 108)

September 7–8, 1863: No Entries

Wednesday, September 9, 1863: *Left our old camp near nicholasville at 12 o clock to day and marched to camp at crab orchard where we are a distance of 13 miles*

35th 1: 1863: ". . . and to Crab Orchard September 9–11."

JQA Journal: (p. 109)

Thursday, September 10, 1863: *Started early this morning and marched about 2 miles beyond Lancaster*

Friday, September11, 1863: *marched to Crab Orchard*

Saturday, September 12, 1863: No Entries

Quincy's Words:

old camp near nicholasville: This was Camp Parke.

crab orchard where we are now: These words were extremely faint but with the aid of *History of the Thirty-Fifth Regiment*, there were enough recognizable letters to complete and confirm this transcription. Similarly, after I had become familiar with the writer's idioms and phrasing, it was much easier to anticipate what he might write; if enough of what could be seen matched positively, the sentences could be completed.

Lancaster: There must have been a store visit or a visit to the local sutler because the ink that Quincy began using on September 9 was far more distinct than that of the previous two weeks.

35th 1: September 13, 1863: **_"Marched over Cumberland Mountains to Knoxville, Tenn."_**

Author's Note: After changing hands several times, the strategic Cumberland Gap was finally surrendered to the Union forces.

35th 2: 1863: "Proceeding to Knoxville, Tenn."

35th 4: September 13, 1863: "The Fifty-first Pennsylvania and the Thirty-fifth received the anticipated order… Over the Mountain! came the call, eight days' rations to be carried by each man… preparation for a hungry land. The number of guns was only about one-hundred at the start so many men were sick or detailed." However, much like their sojourn through the Blue Ridge Mountains the previous year, the autumnal splendor was not lost on the men and noted this and the other pleasantries of the trek in their history. "The way was enliven by the drum and fife, or the bugle echoing from the sides of the hills, calling the halt, or the more unwelcomed signal for forward movement." After reading this I reflected on the many hikes I had taken through the cloves of my own Catskill Mountains in upstate New York, while cloaked in autumn colors. I did not, of course, have to worry about what might await me in the next confrontation with the enemy.

A sutler's establishment in a Union camp. Courtesy of the Library of Congress

JQA Journal: (pp. 110–115)

September 13–30, 1863: No Entries

Elsewhere in the War: September 19–20, 1863: The Battle of Chickamauga: During this time, a major push to disrupt the Union Army's attempt to reach the besieged troops in Chattanooga, Tennessee, is broken up with heavy losses on both sides. Union General George H. Thomas receives the moniker "The Rock of Chickamauga" by holding out against Confederate General Braxton Bragg, thus allowing the Union Army to relocate to Chattanooga.

JQA Journal: (pp. 116–117)

Thursday, October 1, 1863: *Expect to march to morrow at 7 oclock AM*

35th 1: 1863: ". . . thence to Lenoir Station October 1–29"

Friday, October 2, 1863: *started this morning at about Haf 7 1/2 AM and marched about 12 miles over the worst road we ever marched quite tired*

Saturday, October 3, 1863: *Started about 10 AM and marched 5 miles*

Sunday, October 4, 1863: *marched 17 miles passed through mount Vernon yesterday morning*

Monday, October 5, 1863: *Marched 9 miles to day are within 2 1/2 miles of London expect to stop here 2 or 3 days*

Tuesday, October 6, 1863: No Entries

Quincy's Words:

the worst road we ever marched: An excerpt from *History of the Thirty-Fifth:* "The column left Crab Orchard on the second of October, passing over what appeared at that time the roughest road we had ever seen. One of our wagons and one of the Fifty-Firsts got capsized during the afternoon; others stuck in the mud; the work of the teamsters was harder than that of the foot soldiers; the march was twelve miles nearly to Mount Vernon."

35th 4: "On the fifth [of October] there was continued heavy work for the teams, at one place of steep ascent for a mile required a team of ten mules to haul each wagon. The boys, however, feeling frisky, and the mountain air was so bracing that, a mile or so from getting into camp at Pitman's near Loudon, they must needs have a race with the artillery. The men set up a shout, the drivers whipped up their horses, and away we went on the run, 'Hi!—Hi!—Hi!' through the pitch-pine woods and over the sandy roads into the camp of the Eleventh New Hampshire, in a way to scare off whatever malaria still hung about us—that was a jolly race!"

JQA Journal: (pp. 118–119)

October 5–9, 1863: No Entries

Saturday, October 10, 1863: *Left Loudon to day at noon marched 10 miles*

9th Corps: *"Ferrero's Division had a sharp little fight at Blue Springs, Tenn., October 10, 1863. . . ."*

35th 4: "This was the day of the battle of the first Division and the 21st Massachusetts of our old brigade at Blue Springs near Bull Gap. . . ."

Sunday, October 11, 1863: *marched 20 miles to day weather fine*

Monday, October 12, 1863: *16 miles to day Camped just outside Barbourville* ***x**__*

Quincy's Words:

***x**__*: A mysterious "X" followed by an underline was written by Quincy at the bottom of the page. What did it mean?

Author's Note: The recording of the distance marched each day for three days, over hilly terrain, carrying gear, yields a forty-six mile total and attests to rigors of Civil War infantry life.

35th 4: Quincy's Bugle heard? "The march over the mountain was worth making for the pleasure of it alone. The road led through a wild country abounding in natural beauties and wonders. The month was October, the harvest season of the year, and, like our tramp along the Blue Ridge the autumn previous, the route was among hills glowing with resplendent foliage or empurpled by distance. The way was enlivened by the drum and the fife, or the bugle echoing from the sides of the hills, calling the halt, or the more unwelcome signal for forward movement."

35th 4: During these weeks in mid-October there seems to have been considerable cavalry action associated with the war in East Tennessee. The regimental history mentions "the cavalry of the department, both up and down the valley, met with such severe handling that it was drawn nearer to Knoxville; so it appeared that we have arrived just in time for the fun." An observation of cavalry happened on the twenty-second, when the "regiment started for the city, only to enjoy a comfortable sleep upon the platform of the freight-house at the station. It rained in the morning, and the troops crowded into the station, where fires were built between railroad ties, and the men gathered about with steaming overcoats. Mingled with us a lot of East Tennessee cavalry, wild-looking fellows, like Texas Rangers; they had their saddles with them and were waiting for remount. . . . The cavalry, supported by infantry, were somewhere on the south side of the Tennessee, towards a place called Philadelphia, and rumors of the defeat of Woolford's Cavalry . . . found their way into camp."

35th 4: A few days later the dynamic movements of the campaign necessitated a hurried pullback from the south side of the Tennessee River. The history includes a scene that could be right out of a Hollywood movie: "A locomotive and cars had been taken, piecemeal, to the south bank, and put together in running order; there being no time to bring them back, and they must be destroyed. A full head of steam was gathered in the engine, the cars attached, and started for the brink of the abyss where the bridge had been—the driver jumping off and leaving the train to its fate. We were busy upon the river bank when the train was heard approaching the abutment high above us; all looked up and watched for the catastrophe. On came the engine, roaring like a wild bull; it reached the abutment, leaped into the air, and with its cars plunged headlong into the river; the agitated waters foamed and raged, then flowed on as calmly as before. It seemed as if we had witnessed the drowning of a friend. Soon after, a few men in gray appeared upon the southern bank. . . ."

JQA Journal: (p. 120)

Tuesday, October 13, 1863: *Marched 14 miles are within 2 miles of Cumb Gap Am quite sick to night mean to stop at the hospital at the Gap if I can.*

Wednesday, October 14, 1863: *Was left at the port hospital this morning am feeling quite sick*

October 15, 1863: No Entry

JQA Journal: (pp. 121–123)

October 16–24, 1863: No Entries

35th 2: 1863: ". . . which it reached Oct. 22, it participated in the defense of the city [Knoxville, Tenn] against Longstreet."

Author's Note: Confederate General James Longstreet was the longest serving and most reliable of the Southern generals. Lee himself would refer to him as "my old war horse."

Quincy's Words:

Cumb Gap: The Cumberland Gap is a natural pass through the Cumberland Plateau, a mountainous upland of the Appalachian chain, which runs diagonally northeast across the southeastern portion of Kentucky.

Author's Note: Quincy was in the Cumberland Gap hospital from October 15 through 25, a total of ten days. There is no evidence as to his affliction but I suspect pneumonia. Civil War hospitals were a far cry from today's modern medical centers; doctors were relatively few and at least at war's beginning, nurses were not to be found. An understanding of the relationship of germs to disease did not exist and therefore there was no sterilization of medical dressings or any particular attempt at wound cleanliness. The wounded often had to find their own way off the battlefield and to help. At first there were few preparations for evacuation and perhaps only a primitive attempt of triage by the few noncoms available. Eventually musicians were assigned as stretcher-bearers as soon as they were freed up. There were few surgeons and perhaps a few civilian volunteers to care for the wounded after the army moved on. Open fields, barns, tents, or private homes became the hospitals and operating rooms.

When the soft lead of a round musket ball or the higher velocity of the semi-conical Minnie "ball" hit the human body, it created horrific destruction to soft tissue, splintering bones and blowing a massive hole out the rear if it passed all the way through the body. Amputation was the primary treatment for shattered limbs. As horrible and numerous as battlefield casualties were, disease was an even bigger killer of the soldiers. In fact, far more soldiers died of diseases such as measles, mumps, whooping cough, and pneumonia. It is estimated that over twice as many men died of disease than were killed in actual combat. Growing up on farms and in small towns isolated from large populations, many young men had not developed immunities to child-

hood diseases and inoculation was not known. The handling of the wounded improved as the war went on, largely because of civilians such as Clara Barton and Walt Whitman who served as volunteer nurses. When Quincy entered the hospital at Cumberland Gap and again at

A very neat semi permanent Union field hospital utilizing logged-up walled tents. Courtesy of the Library of Congress

Annapolis, there was no guarantee that he would walk out alive, but walk out he did.

JQA Journal: (pp. 124–125)

Sunday, October 25, 1863: *Left the hospital to go to my regt at 2 o clock P.M.*

Monday, October 26, 1863: *Marched 19 miles to last night to within one mile of Tasgsh marched 18 miles to day overtook the 11 N.H. at noon today at the Clinch Rr.*

Tuesday, October 27, 1863: *Marched along with the 11th to day marched 15 miles*

Wednesday, October 28, 1863: *Marched 15 miles to day reached Knoxvile at about 4 PM. going to Loudon to morrow to get my transportation bill*

Thursday, October 29, 1863: *slept in parson Brownlow's psinty office last night reched my regt at about noon 6 miles from Louden.*

Friday, October 30, 1863: *Rained last night not enough to hurt anything, going to be mustered back to morrow*

Quincy's Words:

the 11 N.H.: One of the five regiments of the Second Brigade that had been with them in the Battle of Fredericksburg.

transportation bill: This was a pass authorizing a troop to board a specific railroad train or boat as the case might be.

the Clinch Rr.: **N.G. Map:** The only railroad I could find on the National Geographic Map anywhere near Knoxville in 1863 was labeled the "Virginia & Tennessee R.R.," but the Clinch River runs northeast to southwest, paralleling the Allegheny Mountains just west of Knoxville. This portion of the railroad might have been called the Clinch.

parson Brownlow: "Parson" Brownlow was originally a Methodist circuit preacher whose full name was actually William G. Brownlow. He had become a voice against secession and the Southern cause, spreading his message throughout Eastern Tennessee and beyond by way of a weekly newspaper called *The Whig.* Two other publications of his mentioned in the regimental history were the *Pro-Union Knoxville Whig* and *Rebel Ventilator.* He had been arrested and imprisoned for a time by the Confederate authorities. A passage recounts the parson coming up to meet the troops while they were at the Cumberland Gap: "He was an old hero in our eyes, and when he got out and walked up through the pass the regiment cheered, while the band played patriotic tunes—it was a triumphal welcome home to the redoubtable patriot." (Apparently the regiment now has a band or at least there was one present at the Gap.)

Author's Note: Immediately upon release from the hospital, Quincy, marching alone, covered thirty-seven miles in two days to catch up with the Eleventh New Hampshire. He then marched with them for fifteen miles, and apparently pushed ahead another fifteen miles the next day, and then as calculated on the map, another twenty-six miles to finally catch up with his regiment. In other words: Quincy was released from the hospital and immediately "marched" ninety-three miles in just over three days to get his "transportation bill." This is an impressive feat, especially when considering that this was in contested territory and bushwhackers were known to haunt the area and prey upon stragglers.

JQA Journal: (p. 126)

Saturday, October 31, 1863: *was mustered for 2 months pay hope we shall get it son drew half rations of bread coffee and sugar get meat enough*

Sunday, November 1, 1863: *Cold last night heavy frost warm and pleasant to day drew rations of rice, molasses, and potatoes living high reced a letter from home to night.*

Monday, November 2, 1863: *Weather fine. answered the letter that I reced last night, nothing new   talk of loging our tent up to morrow*

Quincy's Words:

***loging our tent up*:** The tents of the soldiers have been "logged-up" for warmth and extra living space. Several pictures of logged-up tents can be found within these pages.

***living high*:** When "living high" is defined by a diet of rice, molasses, and potatoes, it says a lot about the quality of rations even while in camp.

JQA Journal: (pp. 127–128)

Tuesday, November 3, 1863: *Exceedingly warm repeat-ed that we are going to move in 2 or 3 days Are cutting logs to log up our tent but if we are going to move it wont pay*

Wednesday, November 4, 1863: *Cloudy this morning but warm Sun came out this afternoon and was quite hot got to blow Tatto on the bugles now all the drum heads have burst Co. G. got their boxes this afternoon.*

35th 1: November 4–December 23, 1863: *Knoxville Campaign*

Thursday, November 5, 1863: *Cloudy this morning and looks like rain am feeling much better this morning been raining this afternoon made a requisition for clothing to night*

Friday, November 6, 1863: *Rained hard last night pleasant this morning*

Saturday, November 7, 1863: No Entry

Sunday, November 8, 1863: *Weather fine Leonard is fixing up the end of his tent everything goes along the same as usual*

Quincy's Words:

***got to blow Tatto on the bugles now all the drum heads have burst*:** This would indicate that all of the brigade drummers normally beat out "Tattoo," but because all the drumheads had burst, he and probably others would have to blow "Tattoo" on the bugle. "Tattoo" is the evening call to return to quarters.

Co. G. got their boxes: Food rations were often issued in boxes.

Leonard: This is probably Leonard Boardman (mentioned elsewhere). The following phrase may also imply that it seems like he is *always* fixing up this tent.

JQA Journal: (p. 129)

Monday, November 9, 1863: *Have concluded to fix up our tent and build it higher weather very windy and disagreeable not feeling very well to day*

Author's Note: There is a large ink stain finger or palm print on the journal page here, presumably that of Quincy.

Tuesday, November 10, 1863: *Have got the tent built up been much warmer than yesterday. shall finish our fire place to morrow going to commence laying the pontoon bridge to morrow*

Wednesday, November 11, 1863: *Reveille this morning at 5 o clock went down accross the river after laying round all day drum corps did not have to go*

Quincy's Words:

pontoon bridge: Armies on the move were accompanied by mule-powered wagon trains carrying food, ammunition, and supplies. These trains could stretch for miles along the rough roads of the era. Often army engineers would find it necessary to build their own portable pontoon bridges when existing bridges were inadequate or fords were flooded.

tent built up: This refers to the logging-up process explained earlier, and probably the addition of a stone-and-mud fireplace in winter. Judging by the number of "built-up" tents shown in period photographs, it was a very common practice when camping for extended periods of time at one location. This process essentially produced a log cabin with a tent roof, significantly increasing the headroom. Even the round, tepee-shaped Sibley's tents could be logged up with short, vertically placed cordwood.

JQA Journal: (p. 130)

Thursday, November 12, 1863: *Cold and frosty this morning Luint Tobby came into camp this morning after very man in camp got except the cooks got relieved this noon*

Sure-footed army mules pull heavily laden wagons slowly across a pontoon bridge over an unidentified river. Courtesy of the Library of Congress

Friday, November 13, 1863: *Quite pleasant not feeling very well flour that we draw makes me sick*

Saturday, November 14, 1863: *Had reveille this morning at 4 o clock struck tents as soon as it was light been raining all day lay around in the rain and then put up our tents again*

35th 1: 1863: "At Lenoir Station until November 14."

Author's Note: Lenoir Station, on the East Tennessee & Georgia RR. From Quincy's journal and the generalized histories that abound, it was difficult for me to understand the role of the Thirty-Fifth in this phase of the Tennessee Campaign. The history of the regiment provided an eyewitness perspective, after the fact. The following are abridged excerpts portraying the situation from the Thirty-Fifth's point of view.

35th 4: November 14, 1863: Lenoir Station, Tennessee: "The Confederates, having failed in their efforts to prevent Grant and Thomas from opening railroad connection between Chattanooga and the base of supplies at Nashville, now turned their attention to freeing their own direct communications with Lee's army and Virginia, which our position served. . . . At three o'clock in the morning . . . in the darkness and rain the regiment was awakened and ordered to 'turn out without noise and stack arms on the color line.' The builders had their huts and mud chimneys almost done and were anxious to learn 'What was up,' but the cynics were ready with their 'I told you so'. . . . the tents were left till the last moment on account of the severity of the weather. Soon after, 'Strike tents!' and when this was done down came the rain in a deluge. At daylight . . . the [wagon] trains began moving towards Knoxville . . . wagons, ambulances, artillery and troops, all on the move. . . . This was the scene as we sat on our knapsacks among the ruins of our camp, reading Parson Brownlow's 'Knoxville Whig and Rebel Ventilator'. . . During the afternoon our pontoon bridge . . . was destroyed.

"About two in the afternoon a locomotive came down from Knoxville and stopped in front of us. . . . From the tender jumped General Burnside and Ferrero, and in less than fifteen minutes affairs took a different turn; the fighting portion of the army was faced about . . . towards Loudon. . . . [N]ear sunset a few cannon [shots] were heard. . . . Longstreet was crossing the Tennessee, by a pontoon-bridge at Hough's Ferry below Loudon. . . . It was obvious to us that the enemy must be delayed as much as possible to enable our trains to reach Knoxville and the city to be fortified. He had about three men to our one, so hindering him rather than fighting him was our only prudent course. It has since been stated that, by an understanding between Generals Grant and Burnside, our little army was fronted close to Longstreet to bait him on and draw him so far from Bragg that a return would be impracticable, when the grand battles about Chattanooga should be delivered."

35th 4: November 15, 1863: Lenoir Station, Tennessee. "We were routed out again at half-past one in the morning. . . . [I]n twenty minutes we were upon the road south, towards Loudon. . . . [M]en stumbled upon each other in the darkness, rapping the file leaders over the head with their muskets, or slipped and sat in the mud. . . . At daylight we reached . . . the Tennessee; about ten o'clock the Twenty-First Massachusetts was deployed as skirmishers and moved down the river until they struck the foe, who did not attack us, being intent upon his crossing and seeking to pass by our right-flank to get a start in the race for Knoxville, which he knew to lie open to him. . . . the Thirty-fifth was drawn back out of sight. . . . Meanwhile General White's Division . . . and our First Division had retired to Lenoir's leaving our division . . . to cover the rear. About the middle of the afternoon the Twenty-first came off the skirmish line . . . and we started for Lenoir's at quick time. . . . Reaching the neighbor-hood of the station at dusk, our regiment was deployed as skirmishers, faced to the rear, across the road we had just come over. The position was taken by order communicated through Captain Davis of the Brigade staff, and, as it was known that the enemy was at least abreast of us . . . the arrangement was looked upon as a sacrifice of the Thirty-fifth. It was remarked to the Captain: 'This means that the regiment is to be killed, wounded or taken prisoner'; he replied, 'It looks very much like it, good bye,' and rode off.

"As the men took positions behind rocks and trees, peering into the darkness, the last of the rear guard cavalry rode past, and silence fell on all; the chirp of an insect sounded like the rebel yell, and every foot-fall was the tramp of the advancing enemy. It was uncertain from which the gray-coats might first appear, front, flank or rear. Color sergeant Patch was posted down the road with the colors, with instructions what to do with the flags should the regiment be overpowered. Such moments are trying at the time, but, if the result be happy, are not unpleasant to remember. But a sacrifice was not required. . . ."

JQA Journal: (p. 131)

Sunday, November 15, 1863: *Started at 3 o clock this morning and marched to Loudon this morning marched back to Leniore Station to night kept on for Knoxvile to night*

Monday, November 16, 1863: *Marched all night and made only 3 miles had to go slow on account of the batteries roads very bad had a fight at Cameron Station this afternoon had 3 men wounded*

35th 1: November 16, 1863: Campbell's Station

9th Corps: ". . . and the whole corps was engaged, November 16th, at Campbell's Station."

Tuesday, November 17, 1863: *Marched all night last night reached Knoxvile this morning makes 3 nights we had no sleep to speak of got our tents pitched once more*

35th 1: November 17–December 4, 1863: Siege of Knoxville

35th 4: November 16, 1863: Campbell's Station, Tennessee, ninety miles north of Chattanooga: "The Thirty-fifth formed line . . . north of the road and advanced. . . . [T]he musketry was quite brisk. . . . [S]everal of our men were wounded by shots from the right, but no enemy appeared in our front. . . . With both our flanks resting upon wooded hills, and the guns in position defended by veteran soldiers, became a formidable barrier to Longstreet's progress. . . . the Thirty-Fifth was next, with a skirmish line composed of Companies C, D and K, in front. In this left wing were the guns of Roemer's battery, which did excellent service. To attack us the enemy must come out of the woods and expose themselves to our artillery. From our position we could see both armies, and it was a grand site. The Confederates came out in line with colors flying, fully expecting, apparently, that as soon as they got close to us we would retreat as before; but they were mistaken, for no sooner were they in sight than our batteries poured shells and shrapnel into their ranks with terrible effect; we could see the shells burst among them, and they would break and run for the woods."

Author's Note: By the end of a day of further maneuvering, the objective of delaying Longstreet for twenty-four hours had been met. The Thirty-Fifth and the remainder of the exhausted column arrived in Knoxville on November 17.

JQA Journal: (pp. 132–133)

Wednesday, November 18, 1863: *The sun shone today for the first time for 3 esly days the men are all busy digging on fortifications expect a big battle son*

Thursday, November 19, 1863: *nothing new the rebs thou a few shells over or caissons havnt done much damage yet*

Elsewhere in the War: Lincoln delivers the Gettysburg Address.

November 20–23, 1863: No Entries

Quincy's Words:

caissons: Caissons are a part of the field artillery piece configuration. The unit is made up of a gun, either a smoothbore or a rifle (spirally grooved barrel), and its two-wheeled carriage. When transported, the gun is towed by a two-wheeled limber that is equipped with a harnessing pole and usually pulled by six horses. The limber carries an ammunition box that doubles as a three-man seat. A two-wheeled two-ammunition box cart with spare wheel and seat is hooked to another limber similarly configured. These two wagon-like units are highly mobile and maneuverable. There was a combined seating capacity for the eight-man gun crew; the remaining crew rode team or separate horses. Two guns made up a section; a battery typically had six guns and was commanded by a captain. An artillery brigade normally consisted of five batteries and was commandeered by a colonel.

35th 4: The brigade was stationed in and along these "fortifications" with almost constant threat, exchange of fire by the pickets or testing of the line by the Confederates occurred throughout Thanksgiving week. Food supplies continued to dwindle. The Thirty-Fifth lost only one man killed and one captured, who later died in the prison camp at Bell Isle. This continued through the Thanksgiving period up until November 29.

November 23–25, 1863: The battles for Chattanooga culminated with Lookout Mountain ("the Battle above the Clouds") and Missionary Ridge, forcing a Confederate retreat. These victories opened the "Gateway to the South" and changed the course of the war in favor of the Union.

By this time in my research, I rediscovered a piece of information that the staff at the Antietam National Battlefield had put together for me. A sheet entitled "Battles Involving the 35th Massachusetts Infantry: Campbell's Station, Knox County, Tennessee" now made sense to me. The sheet read:

In early November 1863, Lt Gen. James Longstreet, with two divisions and about 5,000 cavalry, was detached from the Confederate Army of the Tennessee near Chattanooga to attack Maj. Gen. Ambrose Burnside's Union Department of the Ohio troops at Knoxville, Tennessee. Following parallel routes, Longstreet and Burnside raced for Campbell's Station, a hamlet where the Concord Road, from the south, intersected the Kingston Road to Knoxville. Burnside hoped to reach the crossroads first and continue on to safety in Knoxville; Longstreet planned to reach the crossroads and hold it, which would prevent Burnside from gaining Knoxville and force him to fight outside his earthworks. By forced marching on a rainy November 16, Maj. Gen. Ambrose Burnside's advance reached the vital intersection and deployed first. The main column arrived at noon with the baggage train just behind. Scarcely 15 minutes later, had Longstreet's Confederates approached. Longstreet attempted a double deployment: attacks timed to strike both Union flanks simultaneously. Maj. Gen. Lafayette McLaw's Confederate division struck with such force that the Union right had to redeploy, but held. Brig. Gen. Micah Jenkin's Confederate division maneuvered ineffectively as it advanced and it was unable to turn the Union left. Burnside ordered his two divisions astride the Kingston Road to withdraw three-quarters of a mile to the ridge in their rear. This was accomplished without confusion. The confederates suspended their attack while Burnside continued his retrograde movement to Knoxville. Had

Longstreet reached Campbell's Station first, The Knoxville Campaign's results might have been different. Estimated Casualties: 970 total (US 400; CS 570), Results Union victory

JQA Journal: (pp. 134–135)

Tuesday, November 24, 1863: *the rebs made a charge last night and drove in our pickets we made a charge this morning and drove them back the weather is rainy everything quite*

Wednesday, November 25, 1863: *Weather fair and everything quiet*

Thursday, November 26, 1863: *Quite cold last night warm and pleasant to day. Thanksgiving at home We are only half rations every one here is talking about Thanksgiving, wishing they were at hom*e.

Quincy's Words:

the rebs made a charge last night: The Confederates were apparently testing the strength of the Thirty-Fifth's position.

Thanksgiving: In 1863 President Lincoln proclaimed Thanksgiving a national holiday to be celebrated the fourth Thursday in November. Quincy and the Thirty-Fifth "celebrated" this first official Thanksgiving with half rations.

Friday, November 27, 1863: *Warn and pleasant nothing new the rebs are very quiet traded a ration of tabacb for a loaf of bread enough to last a few days*

Saturday, November 28, 1863: *Had some hard fighting last night and this morning the rebs undertook to take Br Benjamin's Battery and were repulsed with great slaughter.*

Quincy's Words:

traded a ration of tabacb: Informal trading between the soldiers of the two armies, though not officially allowed, was a common occurrence during lulls in fighting.

Had some hard fighting last night: This hard fighting was a prelude to the Battle of Fort Sanders the following day.

Benjamin's Battery: Units were commonly referred to by the commanding officer's name. A battery of artillery usually consisted of four to six field cannons. Benjamin's battery was Battery E, Second United States Artillery.

A Union artillery battery typically consisted of six guns, with either smoothbore or rifled barrels. Each gun was attached to a limber and pulled wagon-like by a team of horses. A second limber and caisson accompanied each gun, pulled by another team. All told, they carried four chests of ammunition, and a nine man gun crew. Courtesy of the Library of Congress

November 29, 1863: Battle of Fort Sanders (Fort Loudon)

35th 4: Confederate losses: 800–1,100 killed and wounded, 300–400 prisoners

Sunday, November 29, 1863: No Entry

35th 4: Frank Porter of Haverhill, MA, Company G, killed on picket line, Knoxville.

N.G. Map: This City (Knoxville, Tennessee) was loyal to the Union, but remained in Confederate hands until September 2, 1863, when it yielded to Burnside's advance. (Confederate) General Longstreet's attempt to regain Knoxville ended with a disastrous forty-minute assault on November 29, 1863.

JQA Journal: (p. 136)

Monday, November 30, 1863: *Cold and frosty been building a new tent going to build a fire place to morrow.*

Tuesday, December 1, 1863: *built our fire place got good one some of the musicians are going to work on the fortifications to night.*

Wednesday, December 2, 1863: *everything is quiet weather pleasant*

built a fire place: December in the hills of Kentucky can be quite cold and when troops were camped for more than a few days, rudimentary fireplaces would be built from available materials such as stone, building rubble, or logs with clay mud for mortar and firebox lining. Chimneys were often built with logs, sticks, or wooden barrels with a dried mud lining. The Union field hospital, pictured on page 121 shows neatly logged-up tents, at least one appears to have a well built chimney.

fortifications: Depending on the length of stay and the threat level, temporary fortifications would be built up. There was plenty of manpower to dig mound and trench forts around the camp. Sometimes abatis, treetops with sharpened branches pointing outward, would be set to form an outer defense so as to entangle assaulting troops.

Logged-up and winter-ready tents complete with stone-and-mud fireplaces and vertical stick, mud-covered and lined chimneys. Courtesy of the National Archives

A heavy artillery company is marching out of Fort Slemmer through the fort wall. This and its sister, Fort Massachusetts, were built in defense of Washington. The trench and abatis forming the outer ring of the fort can be clearly seen. Notice the bugler at the head of the line. Courtesy of the National Archives

JQA Journal: (pp. 137–146)

Thursday, December 3, 1863: *Warm and pleasant got only half rations of meal on account of the mill breaking down considerable shelling they are moving their wagon train*

Friday, December 4, 1863: *warm and pleasant*

Saturday, December 5, 1863: *The rebs left last night there have been a number of prisoners brought in Woolford's cavalry are after them got some potatoes this afternoon* [I will] *write a letter home to night*

Quincy's Words:

***half rations of meal on account of the mill breaking*:** Grist mills for the grinding of cereal grains such as wheat, corn, and rye were never located far from human habitation in 1863. Today the majority of our meal and resultant baked goods are typically transported from large mills and bakeries, perhaps hundreds of miles from our local markets. When large armies were encamped, local mills would have been commandeered or otherwise put to use feeding the men. Waterpower was by far the most common source of motive energy. It is also possible that portable horse-powered mills could have been employed when the supply wagons could catch up with the moving army.

35th 2: 1863: "After the close of the siege [of Knoxville],

December 4, the Thirty-Fifth soon proceeded to Blains Cross Roads, where it remained, enduring great privations, until January 1864."

Quincy's Words:

prisoners: Little preparation for the handling and care of prisoners was made, especially early in the war. If a prisoner was lucky, he might be properly exchanged or paroled on the promise not to return to arms. If unlucky, he might end up in one of the notorious prisoner-of-war camps such as Elmira in the North and Andersonville in the South. This was often a de facto death sentence.

Woolford's cavalry: Union Colonel Frank Wolford of the 1st Kentucky Cavalry was an outspoken opponent of Lincoln's policies in Kentucky during the Civil War and was against the enlistment of African American soldiers. His archrival was Confederate raider John Hunt Morgan.

35th 1: December 5–19, 1863: Pursuit of Longstreet

Last Entry: Sunday, December 6, 1863: *Cold and rau this morning looks like rain*

(December 7–31, 1863: No Entries)

35th 3: "... enduring great privations ..."

9th Corps: "This [the siege] was followed by the occupation of Knoxville and the gallant defense against Longstreet's forces, terminating, December 5th, in the defeat and withdrawal of the enemy. The campaign in East Tennessee was a memorable one by reason of the Siege of Knoxville, and the unparalleled privations endured by the men. General Willcox resumed command of the corps on January 17, 1864, relieving General Potter; on the 26th, Parke relieved Willcox, who then took command of the Second Division."

35th 4: *December 1863:* **Christmas with the Thirty-Fifth:** "On the twenty-third there was an alarm ... and the Thirty-Fifth made a reconnaissance, with a section of Edwards battery, two miles out, the First Brigade going still further; but the foe had left. Returning to camp, we commenced to log up the tents and build chimneys of sticks and mud in the old Falmouth fashion. ... Short rations continued; on Christmas Day there was no bread all day, and no other food but fresh beef, issued at evening, for a Christmas dinner; even salt to season it was a luxury. Pickets were kept posted.... [T]his duty had the advantage for foraging, the position was rather sought than avoided, except by the shoeless."

The following are approximate facsimiles of the few pages in the "Memoranda and Accounting" section of the journal upon which Quincy has entered several records.

<u>JQA Journal:</u> CIVIL WAR JOURNAL of JOHN QUINCY ADAMS— 1863 Memoranda and Accounting Pages (p. 147–end, only those which contain Quincy's writing)

MEMORANDA

p. 147 *July 26th/63 recedrecede from Gover'n: pr Pants / Cap / Socks ////*

p. 148 *Leonard Boardman Lawrence Mass Warter Street*

Ephraim A Roberts   West & South Dedham Mass

p. 158 Cash Accounts, January

Clothing recd this year beginning August /63: *1 Wollen Blanket, 1 Linen* [blanket], *1 pr. Socks, 1" shoes, 1 blouse, 1pr. Socks, 1" draws, 1" pants*

Author's Note: Leonard Boardman was the Company I Fifer. He possibly had a brother, Frederick, also Company I, who was a drummer. Both were from Waltham, MA. Ephraim Roberts was also a musician in Company I.

35th 4: "enduring great privations…" "The meat rations were eked out by purchasing liver, hearts and tails; and tripe became fashionable. The poor beef-on-the-hoof starved for days, when slaughtered found to be almost without tallow—even the kidney fat frizzling away to nothing in the frying-pan, Nearly every other day a half-ration of hard bread was issued… Those were tough times, but not discouragement; in this, the inward spirit, our men differed from those heroes of Valley Forge—the prospect before us was brighter and more promising of success."

Author's Note: This miserable situation, known to the regiment and probably the entire Ninth Corps, seemed to begin in early to mid-December 1863, and continued on through their departure in mid-March 1864. It was caused by the season and the inability of the Union logistical organization to provide the many thousands of soldiers marching and camping in foul weather with adequate food, clothing, and shelter. The transportation of these essentials was severely hampered by destroyed railroads and bridges, poor roads, and long distances. Much of the contested land had two armies foraging liberally and destroying stores that could not be removed. The worst of these conditions existed for a month and a half while the regiment was encamped at Blain's Cross Roads, Tennessee.

1864—"THANKS-OF-CONGRESS-SHOES," "STARS AND STRIPES TROUSERS" AND THE TRIP HOME

35th 4: *January 1864:* **New Years with the Thirty-Fifth:** "The year 1864 opened with rain, turning to snow, and the weather very cold. The wind was high, and dodging the smoke of the camp fires was an unending amusement. On the third of January there was no bread . . . two ears of corn on the cob were issued to each man in place of the bread ration; the grinders at the mill thought it a good substitute, but some considered it rather 'mulish' treatment, inquired how long it would be before the order would come to fall in for rations of hay—whereupon 'Fall in for your hay!' became a camp by-word."

35th 4: "*On the eighth of January* the whole country was clothed in a mantle of snow two inches deep. Small-pox was prevailing in the district, and all the men were vaccinated. We had read in our youth of Valley Forge and the dark days of the Revolution, and, outwardly, the scenes about us were a renewal of history. We were probably more stinted for food but rather better clothed than the Continental army, although rags and tatters were conspicuous with us; certainly we were not better shod, and necessity . . . suggested that moccasins would be better than bare feet upon the snow; accordingly, squares of green hide were issued in couples . . . to make into foot-wear . . . and put in mind of the foot of an elephant. The boys called these moccasins 'thanks-of-Congress-shoes,' and their ragged pantaloons 'stars and stripes trousers.'"

35th 4: "**General Longstreet had unexpectedly marched southward** . . . as if to flank us. . . . Keeping along slowly towards Knoxville, we turned off to the left . . . loading muskets, prepared to meet the advancing enemy. They, however, appeared to be in weak force, and, after engaging our skirmishers and finding us ready, declined to come on—a few spent bullets came over and that was all."

35th 2: January 1864: "After various movements to Knoxville, Morristown, and elsewhere the regiment returned to Cincinnati."

9th Corps: General Burnside was again assigned to duty as commander of his old corps, which was ordered to repair to Annapolis, MD, for reorganization.

35th 1: 1864: "Operations in East Tennessee until March 20. Movement to Annapolis, Md., March 20–April 7."

35th 4: At Jacksboro on March 23, the Thirty-Fifth received its first full rations since leaving Crab Orchard in October.

35th 2: 1864: "Here [Cincinnati] April 1, it entrained for Baltimore Md., from whence it took bout for Annapolis."

35th 4: "In Pittsburg, on the fifth, we were served a bountiful collation; mottoes were displayed, 'Welcome to our country's Defenders!' 'Welcome the Ninth!' April 6th, Harrisburg and coffee at the Soldier's Rest. Baltimore in the evening . . . one diary notes, the soldier 'slept in a bed for the first time since leaving home, almost two years ago.'"

April 22, 1864: John Q. Adams receives a Surgeon's Certificate of Disability, the equivalent of a medical discharge.

> "... is hereby Discharged from the service of the United States, this twenty second day of April, 1864, at Annapolis Md. by reason of Surgeon's Certificate of Disability
> (~~No objection to his being reenlisted is known to exist~~ *)" [At the bottom of the page in a very small font:] *This sentence will be erased [in this case crossed out] should there be anything in the conduct or physical condition of the soldier rendering him unfit for the Army}"

35th 4: "*On the twenty Third of April* . . . the Thirty-Fifth took the lead . . . toward Washington . . . [O]n the twenty-fifth . . . it cleared off bright and sunny. Major Wales riding at the head of the regiment, in column with the Ninth Corps, we passed company front through the city . . . sidewalks and even the streets, were thronged with people. . . . The torn colors of the old regiments were continually applauded. . . . At Willard's President Lincoln and General Burnside reviewed the column, and here cheering and enthusiasm were vehement, some of the boys even threw up their caps. Yet there was a deeper feeling under it all, as we passed the streets full of well-fed and well-clothed statesmen, politicians, clerks and civil employees, yes, morituri salutamus! 'O Caesar, we who are about to die salute you!'" The Fifty-Sixth Massachusetts had an excellent band, and for the first time we hear them play the soldiers' chorus from *Faust*: "Glory to those who in battle fall—Their bright deeds can with pride recall."

Quincy's discharge document is here provided for the reader to study. I believe it was also an induction document of sorts for several reasons. The pen and handwriting of the five lines up to "Discharge" and the second paragraph are the same. This is information collected upon enrolling. The pen and handwriting used in the remainder of the first paragraph and the third paragraph and the rank of the signing officer differ, and are information taken upon discharge. This would indicate two different scribes and times. The much-faded commanding officer's signature is that of Nathanial Wales, the regimental commander at Quincy's discharge.

The last signature was that of **General Philippe Regis Denis de Keredern De Trobriand.** My research came up with the following: He was a "Civil War Union Brigadier General. Born in Tours, France, he was married to a New York heiress when the Civil War began. He took out American citizenship and entered the service as Colonel of the 55th New York Infantry, later known as the 'Lafayette Guard'. He fought on the Peninsula in 1862 as a regimental commander and as a brigade commander at Fredericksburg, Chancellorsville, and Gettysburg where he defended Dan Sickles' center at the Peach Orchard. After Gettysburg, not much of the Third Corps was left and was consolidated into the Second Corps where he was assigned another brigade until he was promoted to a division command, commissioned Brigadier General, U.S. Volunteers in January 1864 and then Major General by brevet on April 9, 1865."

)I(

Quincy's father, George Whitfield Adams, traveled from Haverhill, Massachusetts, to Annapolis, Maryland, to be with his seriously ill son in the hospi-

---

* John H. Eicher and David J. Eicher, *Civil War High Commands* (Stanford, CA: Stanford University Press, 2001).

Quincy's discharge document was probably also his induction document.

Headquarters 9th A C.
Annapolis, Md.
April 22, 1864
To be discharged
By command of
Maj. Genl. Burnside
Edward M. Neill
Asst. Adj. Genl.

Respectfully oferred to
Col. Thomas Qt. Mr. Balt Md.
for transportation: there
being no pay owe the
within named solider
on settlement of his afes.
Balt Md   Frs B Waines
May 9th/64 Paymaster
U.S.A.
Genl. De Trobriand

Author's Note:
text and spelling shown as it
appears on the original document

OATH OF IDENTITY.

tal. Not surprising from Quincy's descriptions of life in the Union infantry, he seems to have contracted a pulmonary disorder, presumably pneumonia, serious enough to cause him to be discharged with a rendering of him to be unfit for future military service in the army. As noted before, Civil War statistics show that disease killed more than twice as many soldiers as did combat wounds.

The day after his discharge came through, his father wrote to Quincy's mother, Louisa Adams, to update her and for newspapers to be sent to him. George was apparently well read and quite literate (for his time). I have included his letter here to provide the reader with the experience of reading the letter written in his own hand. He shares with Quincy many of his writing quirks in capitalization, spelling, and punctuation. How many of them are normal for the time and how many are just errors provide an interesting question. I have also provided an easier-to-read transcription to the left.

April 23, 1864: Quincy's father writes home to update Quincy's mother on their son's progress and to make a few requests.

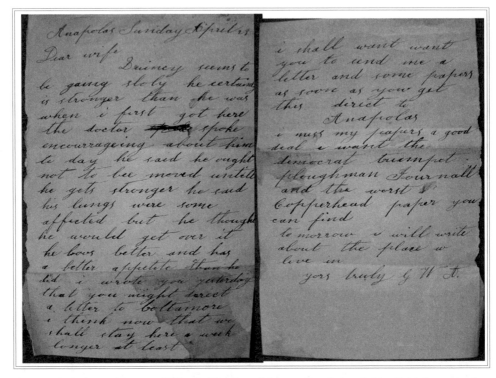

Quincy's father's (George Whitfield Adams) letter dated April 23, 1864, home to his wife, Louisa Morrill Tandy Adams

Annapolis Sunday April 23 [1864]

Dear wife

Quincy seems to be gaining slowly; he certainly is stronger than he was when I first got here. The doctor spoke encouragingly about him today. He said he ought not to be moved until he gets stronger. He said his lungs were some affected but he thought he would get over it. He looks better and has a better appetite than he did. I wrote you yesterday that you might direct a letter to Baltimore. I think now that we shall stay a week longer at least.

I shall want you to send me a letter and some papers as soon as you get this direct to Annapolis.

I miss my papers a good deal. I want the Democrat Trumpet, Ploughman Journal and the worst Copperhead paper you can find.

Tomorrow I will write about the place we live in.

Yours Truly, G. W. A. (George Whitfield Adams)

Quincy's father, George Whitfield Adams, was apparently a regular reader of the *Democrat Trumpet*, probably a relatively conservative newspaper. Lincoln's Republican Party seems to have been the progressive party of the day. If one would compare these to today's major parties of the same names it would seem that they had traded places.

The "worst **Copperhead paper**" would probably have been one of the most conservative, or right wing, of the Democratic Party. "Copperheads" were political activists, and were named for the pins they wore. These were made from the head of Lady Liberty snipped out of the U.S. cent or "penny" of the prewar period of 1793 to 1857. They are known today as "large cents," as they were a little over 1⅛ of an inch in diameter. Liberty's copper head was just the right size for a pin. This handsome coin had its genesis from the British halfpence or "ha'penny," which was modeled after the coinage of the Roman Empire. The King on the halfpenny is even portrayed wearing Roman armor and a laurel wreath, and designated in Latin: GEORGIVS III Rex (King George the 3rd), with seated Britannia on the reverse. After the Revolution, a few states attempted to convert the visage of the King to our George Washington and the goddess Britannia to seated Liberty. We eventually moved her to the obverse and her bust dominated our coinage for years afterward. The U.S. did not go to a small-sized cent until 1856, so there were still lots of these large coins around during the Civil War. I have found many of these but have never found a Copperhead pin. However, another member of my metal-detecting club had.

I have allowed this "Copperhead" side trip because when you are searching for, or researching, a family or adopted hero, you will undoubtedly uncover opportunities for collateral discoveries. If you have made your search a group or family experience, various members might want to pursue these related phenomena according to their own interests. It never ceases to amaze me that when I discover a new connection with the past, it is as though I have opened a doorway leading to a hall containing not only a treasure, but walls lined with more doors, each with another awaiting treasure.

》《

Quincy's father was probably a farmer or from a farming background and most likely had at least a garden. The majority of Americans in 1864 were directly involved in agriculture or at least animal husbandry. The family "car" was a horse and buggy, and the pickup was a farm wagon or buckboard. Although the industrial revolution was underway, for the most part even in

New England, it was still largely an agrarian society. This would explain *The Ploughman Journal*. An Internet search for both newspapers came up empty. However, *Quincy's War* was becoming a family project with my younger brother Mic becoming my proofreader and sounding board. He contacted an old newspaper connoisseur friend of his and he came up with this: "I am still stumped on the *Democrat Trumpet*. However, the *Massachusetts Ploughman*, also referred to as the *Ploughman Journal*, was published in Boston. There were apparently two series: an 1841–1866 series by the Society of Farmers, and a second series, 1866–1906, by the New England Agricultural Society. . . . I did not find it on the Internet archive database. . . . But *Democrat Trumpet* could be a misnomer—e.g., someone calling a paper by its political leaning rather

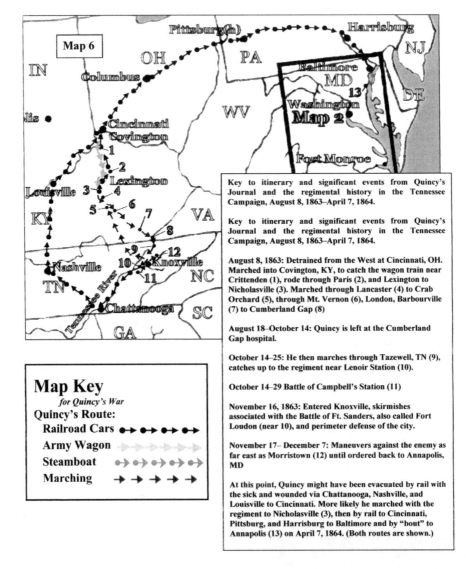

Map Key
for Quincy's War
Quincy's Route:
Railroad Cars
Army Wagon
Steamboat
Marching

Key to itinerary and significant events from Quincy's Journal and the regimental history in the Tennessee Campaign, August 8, 1863–April 7, 1864.

Key to itinerary and significant events from Quincy's Journal and the regimental history in the Tennessee Campaign, August 8, 1863–April 7, 1864.

August 8, 1863: Detrained from the West at Cincinnati, OH. Marched into Covington, KY, to catch the wagon train near Crittenden (1), rode through Paris (2), and Lexington to Nicholasville (3). Marched through Lancaster (4) to Crab Orchard (5), through Mt. Vernon (6), London, Barbourville (7) to Cumberland Gap (8)

August 18–October 14: Quincy is left at the Cumberland Gap hospital.

October 14–25: He then marches through Tazewell, TN (9), catches up to the regiment near Lenoir Station (10).

October 14–29 Battle of Campbell's Station (11)

November 16, 1863: Entered Knoxville, skirmishes associated with the Battle of Ft. Sanders, also called Fort Loudon (near 10), and perimeter defense of the city.

November 17– December 7: Maneuvers against the enemy as far east as Morristown (12) until ordered back to Annapolis, MD

At this point, Quincy might have been evacuated by rail with the sick and wounded via Chattanooga, Nashville, and Louisville to Cincinnati. More likely he marched with the regiment to Nicholasville (3), then by rail to Cincinnati, Pittsburg, and Harrisburg to Baltimore and by "bout" to Annapolis (13) on April 7, 1864. (Both routes are shown.)

than its actual name—as in *Poughkeepsie Republican* rather than *Poughkeepsie New Yorker* because of its political endorsements."

From a personal point of view I am glad Quincy became too ill to continue. Fewer than half of the original enlisted men were left standing in the ranks of the Thirty-Fifth by the end of the war. The others had been killed, died of battle wounds, accident, or disease, or were too sick or disabled to go on. But with an infusion of about five hundred new recruits, the regiment did not take the rest of the war off. It was heavily involved in the campaign in Virginia that led to the Battle of the Wilderness, Second Spotsylvania, and the battle of the North Anna. I have often contemplated the chance of Quincy's survival had he not gotten sick; a thousand bullets and pieces of shrapnel must have flown dangerously close to Quincy. Not to mention surviving the considerable and numerous medical perils that assaulted him, as well as a myriad of other dangers afforded by the long marches and primitive mechanical transportation modes.

35th 4 *Roster:* From December 1863 to September 1864 the regiment had a large influx of recruits. Some were transfers but most were new. The largest number joined in July, Company G receiving sixty-six, of which fifty-seven were German immigrants. The Thirty-Fifth, now close to full strength, would go on to see more serious action. So as not to leave the readers now following the Thirty-Fifth and/or the Ninth Corps without some closure, I include the remainders of their histories.

35th 3: April 1864: ". . . again joined the First Brigade, First Division, IX Corps, Army of the Potomac."

9th Corps: *1864:* "In April, the corps was assembled there [Annapolis, MD], and was composed of the four divisions of Stevenson, Potter, Willcox, and Ferrero, the latter division being composed wholly of colored troops. The corps numbered 19,331, present for duty, with 42 pieces of field artillery; but this number was soon increased, the return of May 10th showing strength of 32,708. In addition to the four divisions, with their two batteries each, there was a brigade of reserve artillery of 6 batteries, and, also, a provisional brigade of heavy artillerymen and dismounted cavalry. In all, there were 42 regiments of foot, and 14 batteries of light artillery. Ferrero's Colored Division had never been under fire, while many of the white regiments in the corps were newly organized, or had served previously on garrison duty only. In the ranks of the old regiments were many recruits and conscripts."

35th 2: 1864: "In the reorganization of the 9th Corps the regiment, now commanded by Major Nat Wales, became a part of Carruth's [1ˢᵗ] Brigade, Stevenson's [1ˢᵗ]
Division. During the battle of the Wilderness, May 5 and 6, and the first part of
that of Spottsylvania,* May 8 to 12, the 35th was in charge of the supply train of
the left Division, and was not engaged. Returning to its brigade, May 17, on the
following day it was in the last assault on the Confederate lines at Spottsylvania,*
moving thence to the North Anna River, where it was again engaged, May 25."

*Spelling is as it appears in this record.

35th 1: May 1864: "Rapidan Campaign May–June. Battles of the Wilderness
May 5–7; Spottsylvania* May 8–12; Ny River May 10; Spottsylvania* C. H.
May 12–21. Assault on the Salient May 12. North Anna River May 23–26.
On line of the Pamunkey May 26–28. Totopotomoy May 28–31."

*Spelling is as it appears in this record.

35th 3: May 1864: "Acting Engineers, IX Corps, to the Army of the Potomac."
This transfer lasted about two months and may have had to do with the
expected digging of entrenchments and siege activity.

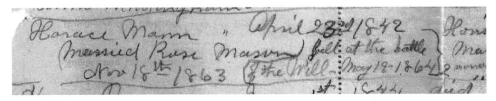

Adams genealogy notes: "Horace Mann [Hunkins] fell at the battle of Will. [Wilder-
ness] - May 19, 1864. Married Rose Mason Nov. 18th, 1863

May 19, 1864: Quincy's would-have-been brother-in-law, Horace Mann
Hunkins, "fell at the Battle of the Wilderness." Had he not been mustered out
a month earlier, Quincy would have been there also. Our family's genealogy
research shows that Horace Mann Hunkins "fell" at age twenty-two on May
19, but the Battle of the Wilderness was fought on May 5–6, 1864. It is possible that the date was confused by later generations, but I supposed that Horace
died thirteen days later from wounds received. Given the medical practices of
the day, it was not uncommon for the wounded to die many days afterward.
Horace had been married to a Rose Mason just six months earlier. Rose would

give birth to their daughter, Horrisa Mann Hunkins, on August 25 of that year.

35th 2: 1864: "It was now detailed as an engineer corps for the 1st Division. At Cold Harbor, June 3, it was posted near Bethesda Church and suffered light loss. Crossing the Jameson June 15, the regiment participated in the siege of Petersburg. At the Crater fight, July 30, it was heavily engaged, losing 12 killed and 34 wounded. At Weldon Railroad, Aug. 19, it was again engaged with loss. It was now reduced to two officers and about 100 men present for duty."

35th 1: 1864: "Cold Harbor June 1–12. Bethesda Church June 1–3. Before Petersburg June 16–18. Siege of Petersburg June 16, 1864, to April 2, 1865. Mine Explosion, Petersburg, July 30, 1864. Weldon Railroad August 18–21. Poplar Springs Church September 29–October 2. Boydton Plank Road, Hatcher's Run, October 27–28."

There were three Hunkins brothers who fought in the Civil War. I found a picture of each. They were unlabeled as so many old photos are; however, I was eventually able to deduce who was who in the Hunkins collection. Pictured here is most certainly Horace Mann Hunkins of the United States First Regiment Heavy Artillery.

9th Corps: 1864: "In the Battle of the Wilderness the corps lost 240 killed, 1,232 wounded, 168 missing; total, 1,640; and, at Spotsylvania, 486 killed, 2,119 wounded, 469 missing; total, 3,146; the heaviest loss at Spotsylvania occurring in the action of May 12th. General Stevenson was killed at Spotsylvania, May 10, and Major-General Thomas L. Crittenden, formerly commander of the Twenty-first Corps, was assigned to the command of Stevenson's [1st] Division. During the Wilderness Campaign, prior to the battle of the North Anna, the Ninth Corps was not included in the Army of the Potomac, but was a separate, independent command, reporting directly to General Grant. This proved to be a faulty arrangement, and so General Burnside, with General Parke, his chief-of-staff, waived the question of their superiority of rank over General Meade, in order that the corps might serve under that officer in the Army of the Potomac. At Burnside's suggestion, an order was issued by General Grant, on May 25th, incorporating the Ninth Corps with the main Army."

The Ninth Corps eventually received its badge. The crossed cannon and anchor were a little more complicated than most of the other lower-numbered corps' badges, which tended to be just basic geometric shapes. Most were of colored cloth shapes sewn on the hat or sometimes the coat. The color of the shield indicated the division within the corps: red for the First, white for the Second, blue for the Third, and green for the Fourth.

Pictured here are the back (left) and the front (right) of a U.S. Eagle Breast Plate, which was excavated many years ago within the Wilderness-Spotsylvania area of conflict. The lead backing is completely melted away, indicating it lay on the ground during a brush fire. Many of the wounded at the Battle of the Wilderness lay in the path of these fires.

9th Corps: *1864:* "On the 9th of June, while at Cold Harbor, General Crittenden was relieved at his own request, and General Ledlie was placed in command of the First Division. In the first assault on Petersburg, June 17th, the corps made a brilliant attack, Potter's Division gaining possession of the works; unfortunately, the division was obliged to relinquish its foothold for want of proper support. The corps was engaged in a similar attempt on the following day, the losses in Potter's and Willcox's Divisions being unusually severe in proportion to the number engaged. Lost, 497 killed, 3,232 wounded, and 262 missing; total, 2,991.

"The enemy's works proving too strong for assault, the army entrenched itself preparatory to the ten months siege which followed. On June 19th, Ferrero's

(4th) Division of colored troops rejoined the corps, having been absent during the whole of the previous campaign, engaged on duty at the rear. Ferrero's men were now placed in the trenches with the other three divisions. The part of the line occupied by the Ninth Corps was very near the enemy's works, and an incessant firing was kept up during the siege, resulting in a daily loss of men, killed or wounded. While there was a comparative quiet in front of the other corps positions, the men of the Ninth were subjected to the terrible strain of a constant watchfulness and deadly exposure. The enemy seemed to be excited to an undue activity by the presence of Ferrero's Colored Division."

In June 1864, Abraham Lincoln wins the nomination of his Republican Party to run for a second term as president. His Democratic rival will be his relieved commander of the Army of the Potomac and now-antagonist General George B. McClellan, whose Democratic Party advocated an earliest possible peace with the Confederacy.

9th Corps: *1864:* "The Ninth Corps was prominently connected with the siege by reason of the immense mine which was dug from within and in front of its line. This mine,* which was excavated by the 48th Pennsylvania, of Potter's Division, was successfully exploded, but the assault which followed was a failure. During this assault Ferrero's colored regiments went into action and fought well, acquitting themselves credibly; their failure, like that of the white regiments in this affair, resulted from causes outside of the regiments themselves. The loss in the Ninth Corps at the mine, was 473 killed, 1,646 wounded, 1,356 missing; total, 3,475. Immediately after this engagement, General Ledlie was relieved from command of the First Division, and General Julius White, of the Twenty-third Corps, was assigned to Ledlie's place."

*This refers to a tunnel that was dug under the Confederate defenses, filled with explosives, and detonated.

35th 3: July 1864: ". . . First Brigade, First Division, IX Corps, Army of the Potomac."

9th Corps: "On the 13th of August, 1864, General Burnside was granted a leave of absence; he never rejoined the corps, but was succeeded by General Parke, who remained in command until the close of the war. At the battle of the Weldon Railroad, August 19–21, 1864, the three divisions of White, Potter, and Willcox were engaged with considerable loss, although the three combined numbered less than 6,000 muskets; casualties, 60 killed, 315 wounded, and els[?] missing. By this time the divisions had become so reduced in numbers that a reorganization of the corps became necessary, and so the regiments in White's Division were transferred to the divisions of Potter and Willcox. Under this arrangement Willcox's Division was numbered as the First; Potter's, as the Second; Ferrero's colored troops were designated as the Third Division. But, in December, Ferrero's Division was permanently detached, and most of his regiments were transferred to the newly-organized Twenty-fifth Corps, which was composed entirely of colored troops. General Ferrero, himself, was assigned to a provisional command at Bermuda Hundred."

9th Corps: "The vacancy caused by detaching Ferrero's Division was filled by six new regiments of Pennsylvanians—one-year men—organized into a division of two brigades, the command of which was given to General John F. Hartranft. This division rendered gallant service at Fort Stedman, and Hartranft added to his laurels by the ability displayed at that critical juncture."

35th 2: 1864: "In another reorganization of the 9th Corps early in September it was assigned to Curtin's (1st) Brigade, Potter's (2d) Division. About this time there were added to the regiment 385 German and French substitutes, recently arrived in this country and ignorant of the English tongue. Major Hudson now commanded the regiment. At Poplar Spring Church, Sept. 30, it was severely engaged, losing 163 prisoners. For two months it was now posted near Forts Fisher and Welsh."

November 8, 1864: Aided by General William Tecumseh Sherman's capture of Atlanta, Lincoln wins a second term as president.

35th 1: 1865: "Fort Stedman March 25, 1865. Appomattox Campaign March 28–April 9. Assault on and fall of Petersburg April 2. Occupation of Petersburg April 3. March to Farmville April 4–10. Moved to City Point, thence to Alexandria April 20–28, Grand Review May 23. Mustered out June 9, and discharged from service June 27, 1865. Regiment lost during service 10 Officers and 138 Enlisted men killed and mortally wounded and 1 Officer and 100 Enlisted men by disease. Total 249."

35th 1: 1865: "During the midwinter it was stationed in the rear of Fort Sedgwick [Fort Hell]. From March 7, 1865, until the fall of Petersburg, April 2, it formed a part of the garrison of this fort. It then joined in the pursuit of Lee's army and was at Farmville when the news came of the surrender. Arriving at Alexandria, Va., April 28, it remained as a part of the garrison of the District of Columbia until June 9, when it transferred its recruits to the 29th Regiment and was mustered out of the service. Returning to Readville, Mass., on June 27, the men were paid off and discharged."

9th Corps: 1865: "The morning report for March 31, 1865, showed a corps strength of 18,153, 'present for duty, equipped,' and 36 pieces of light artillery. With this force the Ninth Corps entered upon the final campaign, taking a prominent part in the storming of Petersburg, April 2, 1865, which resulted in the evacuation of Richmond and the downfall of the Confederacy. The corps was not only among the foremost in this brilliant assault, but its flags were the first to wave over the public buildings of Petersburg. This was the last battle in which the corps participated, and on July 27, 1865, the existence of the Ninth Corps was officially terminated."

These two flags were probably those carried home by the returning regiment after the war. They proudly display the campaigns and battles in which the unit participated. Courtesy of the Massachusetts Art Commission.

April 14, 1865: President Abraham Lincoln is assassinated in Washington, D.C.

By mid-May 1864, Quincy would have been home in Haverhill, Massachusetts, and recuperating. It was evident that his close and loving family was available there to help him. I believe the fourth of Quincy's pictures in uniform was taken at this time. This second tintype with bugle was not peeling like the first, but was heavily scratched and very dark. I would need to do some digital work on it to improve the image for study. I undertook to enhance this photograph as I had done with the journal, using only the photo programs that came loaded in my PC.

A few years earlier I had made a special trip to visit my aunt and photograph as much of the Adams family genealogy collection as possible, before it was dispersed any more than it already had been. I especially wanted to document and digitally capture all the family photographs and in particular those of Quincy in uniform. All together there were four: three that my aunt Barbara had, and the fourth being the one I discovered in the Hunkins collection my cousin Ginny had been keeping. During this process, and the subsequent study, I had taken a closer look at the second photo of Quincy with his bugle. I had always taken the family's word for it that it was Quincy. It did sort of look like him but it was very dark. The person was in a blue uniform and he was posed with a bugle, but was it Quincy? Even though my aunt had verified that this photo had been in her family, and had kept it with Quincy's things since her youth, I decided to try a little "photo forensics."

I first photographed the framed picture as I found it. It had a common brass frame of the type that could be placed right on the photo with or without protective glass. This photo had either lost its glass or never had one. Consequentially, it had several severe scratches marring the upper half of the image, making it even more difficult to identify the subject in the photo.

Left: The second tintype of Quincy with his bugle in its present condition Right: The

same photo without its frame and with light cleaning, showing scratches and staining

I removed the photo from the frame and photographed it again (picture 2). It was a tintype, a common photographic type of that time. Since a tintype is an image in albumen on a black japanned (enameled) piece of galvanized sheet iron (tin), it is easily scratched, and in this case further faded or darkened by exposure. The tintype processes resulted in a positive black-and-white image. Tintypes were sometimes touched up with color paint to enhance their appeal, but this would not necessarily be true color. This photo showed obvious blue color on the pants and gold on the bugle and buttons. Often the buttons are painted with just a touch of paint and appear as gold smug under the magnifying glass. So actually the pants and jacket would not even have to be that of a uniform, just painted to appear to be. However, in this case I had no reason to believe that this wasn't a uniform coat. The actual color of Quincy's bugle, however, is pewter.

Left: Photo after digital enhancement Right: Photo after digital repair of scratches

At a later time I made a digital copy of this frameless photo (picture 3). I then enhanced it several times in the same manner that I did with the journal pages, and I ended up with a much lighter and more recognizable picture of my subject. I then used my older PC, which had an off-the-shelf photo program in it, to copy a small portion of the picture next to a missing piece and pasted it over the spot. Repeating this as many times as necessary, I was able to gain a fairly accurate facsimile of its original appearance (picture 4).

This done, one of the first things I noticed was a somewhat receding hairline. I suppose war could do that to a fellow, but he does look to be several years older than twenty. He also looks well fed. This alone convinced me that this was a postwar pose. As proven by the journal, he had marched a considerable number of dirt-road miles. Somewhere in the neighborhood of a thousand map miles, not counting the ups and downs and the innumerable miles around camp, drilling, and maneuvering in action.

This eventually led me to conclude that it was taken after his discharge and some heavy-duty rest and home cooking during the recovery from his pulmonary distress. We believe that he brought his bugle home and presumably his uniform coat among other things. The color present in one of the photos had been painted on. The blue pants could have been any pants, but the coat appears to be right. The buttons were usually touched up with a dab of gold paint on tintypes but probably not often on glass plates. The bugle was a brass color but this is also painted.

  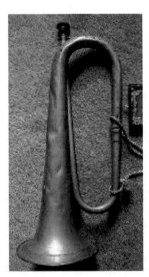

Left: Quincy's bugle, photo May 1, 1863; Center, ca. 1864(?); Right, ca. 2010.

Quincy's bugle is a pewter color. Or was this even Quincy's bugle or a studio prop? I thought I would try a little more forensics to answer the question. There was one other photo of Quincy sitting with his bugle, and I had taken several photos of the bugle, which is in possession of the family—that wonderful bugle of my youth.

By cropping, resizing, and rotating, I was able to line up the three bugle photos so as to be able to compare the two known photographs of Quincy-with-bugle and the actual bugle. Given the various camera lenses used and the shot angles, the proportions were close enough that they could be the same bugle. They all appear to conform to U.S. regulations. The mouthpiece configurations are the same but appear to be of different lengths in each photo. However, by holding a reproduction Civil War–era bugle at various forward angles, the mouthpiece could be made to appear shorter or longer. The modern photo of Quincy's bugle is tipped slightly back from the ventricle by the position of the camera. The bugle in the period photos seems to be tipped forward, and when I sat straight-backed and held the reproduction in the same manner, it naturally tended forward. This test, while not positively proving a match, provided no evidence to suggest they were different bugles. Also, the bands formed where the two tube sections are connected together are just barely visible in both vintage bugles. Actually, I had hoped I would be able to positively match one or more of the dents, which would be as unique as a fingerprint. I considered the possibility of Quincy using a studio prop, but I suspect that he was accustomed to keeping his bugle close at hand. There is always the probability that Quincy had more than one bugle during his tour of duty. It would not be unheard-of for a bugle to be lost or damaged and replaced in two years of marching, camping, and fighting. This little adventure in detective work was interesting and served to confirm in my mind that this is the bugle carried by Quincy in battle, as the family has always known.

Louisa Morrill Tandy Adams, Quincy's mother, taken about the time of his tour of duty or just afterward

QUINCY POSTBELLUM

By April 1865 Quincy would have been well on the road to recovery and ready to get on with his life. Having had pneumonia myself, I know it is a serious disease and can easily turn fatal. The last tintype of Quincy with his bugle (page 153) shows a well fed and healthy young man. Mom's home-cooked meals and the family's first-class care surely facilitated a complete recovery. Certainly he was nursed back to full health by his family, but little else is mentioned of them in the family archives. The most revealing look into his father's life was the letter home from Annapolis. There are only two pictures of Quincy's mom that I am aware of; both show a woman whose handsome features are locked in a somber countenance, perhaps caused by some unspoken sorrow. When I look into her seemingly sad, thoughtful expression, captured on film, I wonder if she felt caught between her father's world and the world of Protestant New England. Or am I looking into the eyes of one of a hundred thousand soldiers' mothers whose constant worry had taken over the resting face? Whatever their stories, Quincy was able to grow to maturity and become the loved and revered grandfather of a large clan of descendants.

There is little actual evidence in the family record of Quincy's life until his later years. Mary, the girl so often mentioned in his journal and the recipient of the "Bound for Memphis" letter, eventually married Quincy's brother, Frank. Presumably Quincy immediately got back to his music and soon took a job as a music teacher. Quincy would eventually publish at least one piece of music called "Buoyancy," a copy of which was in *A Collection of Instructive and Amusing Pieces for the Piano*, published by Theo Presser of 1704 Chestnut Street, Philadelphia, Copyright 1890. My younger brother played this piece on his piano and liked it. Jay Ungar, of *Ashokan Farewell* fame, also played it, proclaiming it "very nice."

December 13, 1875: Quincy at thirty-one years of age married Miss Ellena Wright Hunkins. "Ella" was a local girl, almost thirteen years his junior. They were married by the pastor of the Wesley Methodist Episcopal Church of Haverhill. Four years later she would give birth to Herbert Carroll Adams, who was to be their only child.

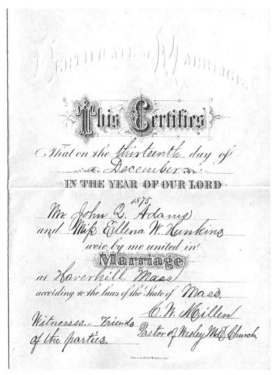

Marriage certificate of John Q. Adams and Ellena W. Hunkins

This albumen print of Ellena W. Hunkins was taken in a Haverhill studio about the time of her marriage to our John Quincy Adams.

Ellena's name seems to morph over time and from document to document: Ellena on the marriage certificate, Eleana on the quitclaim deed and genealogy research, Elena and Ella on photo labels, Nellie in later letters, and Eleanor on the Memorial Resolution and finally on the gravestone. This made tracing her interesting to say the least, but there were many documents and artifacts to cross-reference and an aunt to confirm this. It is not always easy to trace the history of a person whose family did not preserve his or her documents and artifacts, as was the case with Quincy. However, it can be done to some extent by accessing legal documents filed in the various municipal depositories along the route of a person's life. It is my experience in working on other projects that deeds, tax records, wills, and maps are especially helpful and usually easy to access if the county, city, and township where property was owned by the person are known. People did not move around then as much as today and if they owned real property, deeds are your best sources. If they served in the military, these records are also available. In my County Clerk's hall records, most of the newer documents are in a microfilm storage format, but the oldest handwritten and typewritten documents have been copied and are easily accessed and recopied. These make excellent teaching documents for you teachers and parents looking for interesting research for students and children of all ages.

Dateable records are great to find, but many if not most of the older Adams photos have no dates or even the names of the subjects. Some were simply labeled "Grandpa" or "Mom." Not until the Adams sisters began their genealogical project did that problem begin to be rectified. Official documents such as Quincy and Ellena's wedding certificate almost always have dates, but there are exceptions, as I was to find out. Several years ago I was able to develop a fairly comprehensive history of the old road on which I live, based on deeds, wills, and old maps that I found in our County Clerk's hall of records. All were replete with dates. Surprisingly, the quitclaim deed that I found among the Quincy treasures had no apparent date. It appears to be transferring several large parcels of land, including the Haverhill house in which Ellena and Quincy were living, upon the death of her father (Ensign Sargeant Hunkins) and after her marriage to Quincy. Furthermore, it does not describe the properties or

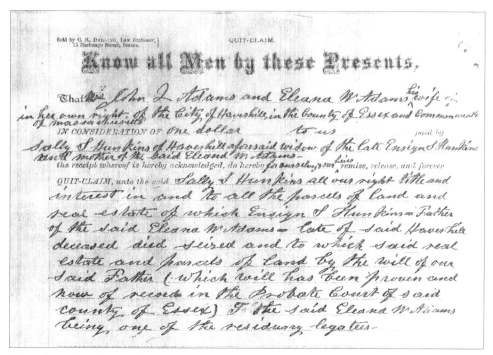

Quitclaim deed transferring the Hunkins home to John Q. and Ellena W. Adams, here spelled Eleana

their location(s). I choose to include it here, again for the experience of the reader. Unfortunately, a copy of the reverse is missing or was blank.

This document appears to have been written by Ellena's brother Ensign Lewis Hunkins, as it states "by the will of *our* said father." As the oldest of the surviving brothers, Ensign Lewis had assumed the role of patriarch of the Hunkins family. This might explain why he had signed as "Father" for his brother, Harry Truman's, final payment.

Quincy and Ellena are married at this time, but she is listed as "Eleana W. Adams" and they are living in the residence ("*residuary* legatees"). There is a residence involved as it makes the distinction "parcels of land *and* real estate." The property is undoubtedly the home and farm of Ellena's mother and father in Haverhill, Essex County, Massachusetts.

After the war Quincy's new brother-in-law, Ensign Lewis Hunkins, would be the only one of Ellena's brothers still alive to appreciate the reunion of the United States. He would leave his commission, become a businessman, move to Aspen, Colorado, and start a jewelry business.

Left: A mustachioed Ensign Lewis Hunkins after the war Above: An envelope mailed from Ensign to his mother, Sally S. Hunkins, at the Haverhill address. It has been used as scratch paper and the stamp has been removed probably for someone's stamp collection.

Quincy and Ellena's only son, Herbert Carroll Adams, would work his way through Dartmouth College in Hanover, New Hampshire, by working construction. I recently inherited his *Scientiae Baccalaurei*, his Bachelor's of Science "sheepskin" or diploma. Today a "sheepskin" is a euphemism for a diploma for a college degree. Herbert's diploma is actually written all in Latin on a real sheepskin parchment. Dartmouth is one of the oldest American colleges, and the smallest of the Ivy League schools. Dartmouth College was established by a charter conveyed by King George III of Great Britain on December 13, 1769, "for the education and instruction of Youth of the Indian Tribes in this Land . . . and also of English Youth and any others." It was a family tradition, by way of my mother, that Herbert's acceptance to Dartmouth was possible, in part, by his one-eighth Native American heritage.

"Granma and Grandpa" Adams, as my mother called them, settled into their lives on the place in Haverhill, and awaited Herbert to produce heirs to his line of the New England Adamses. That was not to be, at least as far as the Adams name goes, as one by one Herbert and his bride, Sylvia Turner Adams,

Quincy and Ellena's only son, Herbert Carroll Adams, in his Dartmouth years

produced four girls. This meant the end of his branch of the Adams name, but it was wonderful for lots of great-grandchildren.

The memory of the other Hunkins brothers would all but fade from the collective family knowledge, saved only by my mother and her sister's genealogy research. Dutifully recorded and stored in a shoe-box file, it was rediscovered by my generation upon the aging of Quincy's granddaughters. The shoebox file was a typical storage format for the day, but highly susceptible to loss or destruction over time. It now fell to my generation to utilize new technologies to collect, organize, preserve, and transfer it to digital format, and thereby make it available to future

Quincy and Ellena in the prime of life living in Haverhill, MA, ca. 1880–90

generations, family, researchers, and in the case of Quincy and the Hunkins brothers, to the growing number of folks interested in the American Civil War.

The last photo I found was hiding between the pages of barely associated material, almost a year after first receiving the genealogy files. It was in a small magenta-colored folder. On the cover was stamped: "N. S. Leeman, Photographer, Cer. Merrimac and Pecker Street, Haverhill, Mass." Opening the folder I was amazed to see an oval matted CDV of the bust of a handsome young solider dressed in a uniform jacket. On the back was printed "W. H. Lane, 4 How St., Haverhill Mass." I felt as though I had seen this young man before. It didn't look like Quincy, so was this one of the Hunkins boys? If it was, why wasn't it with the material I received from Cousin Ginny?

This photo was in the group of material I had received from my aunt Barbara, who had Quincy's memorabilia, but it wasn't Quincy. I had seen that face before. Could it be Horace Mann Hunkins, the boy who "fell" in the Battle of the Wilderness? I went to the picture file to find Horace's digitalized tintype and made a copy, then cropped and pasted it next to that of the newly found CDV. It was Horace! His sister, Quincy's wife, Ella, must have kept it, eventually to be passed down with the Quincy material.

The photo above is most certainly that of Horace Mann Hunkins, who "fell" in the Battle of the Wilderness. It is accompanied by its reverse label and folder cover.

Ellena had not forgotten him but upon her passing, the last of her line, his memory faded quickly, as did that of his younger brother who died at Baton Rouge. This would be the fate of the memory of tens of thousands of Civil War veterans. Perhaps Quincy, through his story, can help to preserve the memory of these boys and the sacrifices they and their comrades made.

QUINCY AND THE GRAND ARMY
OF THE REPUBLIC (G.A.R.)

I t is clear to me that Quincy's war was always with him, and that except for his family, was the defining feature of his life. He had indeed become a true family hero, especially to his four grand-daughters, judging by the volume of keepsakes and the reverent manner with which they spoke of him. They were the keepers of his memory in my growing years. The care and respect they showed for all things "Quincy" serves as a centerpiece for the other aspects of the collective family memory. Fortunately for this story, a considerable volume of memorabilia was generated by this later phase of his life, making for a fitting final chapter. It would seem that his adoring grandchildren had saved everything.

Quincy was an active member of the G.A.R. (Grand Army of the Republic) throughout his senior years. Many of the letters we

Quincy, in his mid forties or early fifties, is seen here sporting the look of the day for mature men. The frame is of note for its military motif. The frame and tintype it has held for a century and a quarter are in very good condition. ca. 1885–95

found preserved among the stack of other memorabilia attest to his involvement and his need to return to the hallowed ground of his past. I have included sections of several that display this importance.

The G.A.R. was the major Union veterans' group after the American Civil War. It was established within a year of the war's end on May 30, 1865, known today as Memorial Day. Organized originally as a Union veterans' group, it quickly became an extremely strong political advocacy group, reaching a membership of over 400,000 prior to the turn of the century. Its members were instrumental in the election of their old commander in chief, Union General Ulysses S. Grant, as president of the United States; four more of its members would also achieve the presidency. Throughout its history, membership was only allowed to "veterans of the late unpleasantness." Its last member died in 1956.

The Grand Army of the Republic had become the focal point of Quincy's connection with this part of his life, and his involvement is well represented in the memorabilia preserved by the family over the years. They seem to speak for themselves, and I decided to share them in a scrapbook format. As before, the actual documents are presented for the reader's experience. They are accompanied with transcriptions only slightly edited to facilitate reading but still preserve the flavor.

G.A.R. uniform buttons recovered by the author in Ulster County, New York

When I first began this project I knew what the G.A.R. was . . . sort of, mostly from reading about the few artifacts I had recovered from local backyards. These, as with all recoveries, would open yet another doorway. Each recovery would have a story to tell and/or mystery to solve. In my career as an outdoor educator we called the opportunity provided by a discovery, a "teachable moment." I guess then, a personal discovery or recovery of an artifact could be called a "learnable moment."

Opportunities for making firsthand recoveries of real artifacts are finite and not readily available to most folks these days. However, opportunities for the discovery of an artifact through flea markets, yard sales, old attics, antique and secondhand shops, or e-trading sites are perhaps better than ever and can provide an endless resource for exploration, discovery, and learning.

Before I made my first G.A.R. artifact find, I had only a passing interest in the organization. My first recovery of a G.A.R. item was a five-point brass star. At first I thought it was a toy sheriff's badge, but it nonetheless sent me to the artifact books. I soon realized that another artifact from the same site was actually related and that they were the remains of a G.A.R. badge. I had just opened a doorway to a whole new area of interest and learning.

My metal-detecting buddy, Kevin, took me to meet a friend of his named Al, and to look at his collection. I quicky decided he must be our regional guru-of-the-G.A.R. He had assembled a museum-quality array. I had previously found a good picture of a complete G.A.R. membership badge for a visual comparison with the badge "skeleton" I had found, but I preferred to use a photograph that I had actually taken myself. Al had a beautiful specimen that he graciously agreed to let me photogarph. In fact, I was overwhelmed by the breadth and quality of material he had collected over a lifetime of studying the G.A.R. His collection contained not only hardware such as medals, badges, and pins, but "softerware" as well in the form of books, records, letters, and various other documents. Many of these he had salvaged from imminent destruction. Truly, it was a collec-

Metallic portions of a G.A.R. badge recovered by the author in Ulster County, New York

tion worthy of its own book. I could not resist presenting a small sampler for my readers.

After examining the medal that I had found, he helped me understand its symbolism. The pendant portion is a five-pointed star with each point ending in a club-like finial bearing another smaller five-pointed star. Beneath each star is an emblem symbolizing the various branches of the military. The sabers represent the cavalry, the muskets and hunting horn represent the infantry, crossed cannons represent the artillery, and an anchor represents the navy. In the center is Lady Liberty representing loyalty to the cause. By her sides stand a soldier and a sailor clasping hands in fraternity.

The complete G.A.R. medal from Al's collection

The two children represent charity. The American eagle and fasces symbolizing strength through unity are backed with U.S. flags and serve as supporters.

To give the reader an idea of some of the kinds of G.A.R. material that was produced for its membership, my new friend Al allowed me photographic access to his collection. He has concentrated on the Hudson Valley community of Rhinebeck, New York. Another by-product of my research is meeting new folks with shared interests.

This is but a sample of some of Al's spectacular G.A.R. collection. Collectors such as this do a great service to the preservation of our shared history. His collection includes, among other things: buttons, badges, pins, reunion ribbons, hat patches, and printed material. Many are attributable to the Armstrong Post No. 104 of Rhinebeck, New York.

Present in the collection is a "first day of issue" three-cent stamped envelope, three cents being the standard first-class letter price in 1949. The old veteran shown on the stamp is wearing a regulation G.A.R. hat like that of Quincy's. This hat shows a crown shaped like that of a civilian hat of the day and provided a clue as to how Quincy's hat may have looked in use.

When Al showed me his library, one old book caught my eye immediately. It displayed a brass bugle that practically leaped off the spine. It was an original copy of the *History of the Grand Army of the Republic,* by Robert B. Beath, published in 1889, Bryon & Taylor, New York. As I continued to scan the other titles on the shelf, I asked Al if he had any information regarding monuments, tablets, or other Massachusetts G.A.R. memorials. He reached up and pulled a volume off the shelf just before my eyes arrived on the spot and handed me an equally venerable-looking volume entitled *Monuments, Tablets or Other Memorials Erected*

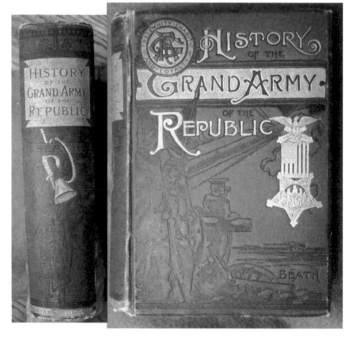

Posed here are two views of the cover of the History of the Grand Army of the Republic, by Robert B. Beath, displaying the brass bugle that "practically leaped off the spine" to catch my eye.

in the State of Massachusetts to Commemorate the Services of Her Sons in the War of the Rebellion 1861–1865. Amazingly, the second page I opened to had a photo of the large G.A.R. monument built in Quincy's hometown of Haverhill. The text next to the picture proclaimed: "Haverhill (Essex County). – When only one of the many Towns in old Essex, Haverhill was the birth place of John G. Whittier, whose trenchant pen and rhythmic voice did so much for the Union and liberty. In 1869 the city dedicated her beautiful monument, at a cost of $6,573. The occasion has long been memorable in local annals. The Major How Post 47 considers its most precious relic the home-made flag borne by the Hale Guards at the first call for troops. In those days bunting was scarce, and the company had no colors, hence Mrs. Nancy Buzzell, a patriotic seamstress, using strips of ribbon in her possession, sewed continuously from Wednesday to Friday noon, with only two hours' sleep, that the soldiers might have a flag under which they could march. In some way the flag was lost in the hurly-burly of war times, and for forty-one years the good lady looked in vain for the object on which she had labored so diligently. At last it came to light and was passed back to the maker, who in 1904 turned it over to the Post, to be cared for, it is hoped, until the last man is mustered out...."

Quincy was a longtime member of Major How Post 47, but ended his years in Post 50, Peabody, Massachusetts.

Later, I couldn't help but reflect on what an exciting experience discovering Quincy's story had been. A map of my quest would look like a huge four-dimensional tree with many branches spreading from its trunk, each branch leading to yet smaller branches and spreading back in time, each twig leading to another discovery. While the American Civil War had been the largest limb in Quincy's life,

The Grand Army of the Republic monument in Haverhill, Massachusetts, as identified in *Monuments, Tablets and Other Memorials Erected in the State of Massachusetts* **Courtesy of the Commonwealth of Massachusetts**

it was not the only one. It is my hope that readers of *Quincy's War* will be inspired to begin their own ancestor discovery quest.

The personal connection notwithstanding, Quincy's G.A.R. memorabilia, while not as spectacular as Mister Coon's, is an important part of telling his story.

A superb painting of Quincy in his G.A.R. uniform adorns the inside cover of *A History of the Civil War 1861–65 and the Causes That Led Up to the Conflict* by Benson L. Lossing. The book was presented to Quincy sometime between 1927 and 1931, probably by members of his G.A.R. post.

The G.A.R. was organized into "departments" at the state level and "posts" at the community level. There were posts in every state in the U.S. at that time, and several posts overseas. Military-style uniforms were often worn by its members.

Quincy was definitely active in veterans' activities, the earliest evidence of which was provided by the discovery a spectacular red ribbon among his treasures. It was from a reunion of the old Thirty-Fifth on September 17, 1891, the twenty-ninth anniversary of the Battle of Antietam. The earliest the Thirty-Fifth Massachusetts Regiment could have held a reunion would have been 1866, but it would take time for physical and emotional wounds to heal before nostalgia could set in. Quincy would probably have joined the Regimental Association at its formation and the G.A.R. shortly thereafter. Another treasure was in the form of a newspaper clipping headlined as "Veterans of Co. G Gather for Reunion." It had "Sept 1927" handwritten along the edge. The date is verified by implying *sixty-five years* after the battle of South Mountain. It goes on to state … "Comdr. Monk had just returned from the national encampment of the Grand Army in Grand Rapids, Mich." My new G.A.R. friend Al later confirmed this encampment was on September 11–16, 1927.

The hand colored photograph of Quincy in his G.A.R coat that adorns the inside front cover of his copy of Benson J. Lossing's *A History of the Civil War*, 1907, dedicated to Quincy, probably by the members of G.A.R. Post 50 (How Post), ca. 1927–1931

At this time Quincy would have been eighty-three years of old. This Haverhill newspaper article headlined "Veterans of Company G Gather For Reunion." The article reads: "Mr. Adams, a former piano teacher, played yesterday for the singing of 'Marching Through Georgia,' 'The Battle Hymn of

Quincy's G.A.R. belt buckle in heavy cast brass is the style and size of so many military plates of the day.

the Republic' and 'My Country 'Tis of Thee.' Mr. Adams now makes his home in Rowley [MA] and motored here yesterday for the reunion." Present were the last four members of Co. G: William Dresser, age eighty-nine; M. L. Stover, age eighty-nine; and George W. Heath, eighty-seven. Quincy looks rather frail here but he is still driving at eighty-three! Mr. Dresser and Mr. Stover were wounded at Antietam. Dresser lost his leg and both mustered out on account of disability that winter (1862-3). Mr. Heath mustered on disability that December as well.

In that same year, Quincy was reveling in his four beautiful granddaughters. He wrote to the family and even to each granddaughter frequently. They lived in Elmira Heights, New York, while he still lived in Massachusetts. Many of these letters survived the years as keepsakes and are now a view into his

Quincy's ribbon for the Thirty-Fifth Regiment's reunion on the twenty-ninth anniversary of Antietam, the Thirty-Fifth's most epic battle

Quincy's hat badge with the post number emblazoned within a wreath. Post 50 was in Peabody, MA. Quincy must have joined this post shortly after he moved to Rowley before 1927. The hat could predate that move, as the post number is interchangeable. Notice that the five is larger than the zero.

person.

Quincy mentions wanting to return to Fredericksburg and Antietam in several letters written to my mother, Ellen, his granddaughter. They are all typically undated, and usually begin simply with "Monday Morning." These visits were to revisit places where hugely significant events in his life took place, and undoubtedly brought back memories of long-lost but not-forgotten comrades. The discovery of a photo of Quincy standing near the granite monument at Burnside Bridge, over Antietam Creek, was identified by our locating the same monument eight decades later. The monument was originally placed on the southeast corner of the bridge. Each of the four regiments of the Second Brigade of General Burnside's Ninth Corps had a monument on a corner of the bridge. They

Quincy's four granddaughters, left to right: Barbara, Virginia, Ellen (author's mother), and Alice

were removed to their present location on the northeast side of the bridge when it was to be restored to its appearance at the time of the battle. This is the same monument that we had found on our pilgrimage to discover Quincy at Antietam. The photo had been roughly cut to fit an oval frame, thus removing enough of its surroundings so

EXCERPTS FROM QUINCY'S LETTERS TO THE AUTHOR'S MOTHER, CA. 1925.

Monday A.M.,

Dear Folks

. . . and then go on to Washington and we could go to Sharpsburg i.e. Antietam and stay overnight and be there for two days and have one of those days be the 17th of September. They always have a celebration on that day and there are always some union and confederate veterans there at that time.

Lots of Love, Father.

Monday P.M.,

Dear Folks

. . . I want to go to the Antietam battle-field once more and have more time to look around and see and I also want to go to Fredericksburg. That is about half way from Washington to Richmond.

Lots of love from Father

Seen here is Quincy standing next to the monument to the Thirty-Fifth Massachusetts as originally placed by Albert Augustus Pope on the northwestern corner of Burnside Bridge at Antietam. The monument was later moved to its present location in preparation for the bridge being returned to its 1862 appearance.

that I was unable to identify its location until after our trip to Antietam.

Assigning dates to undated letters and newspaper clippings can be an interesting challenge. Someone had written the date on a 1927 newspaper article and accompanying picture of the last four survivors of Company G. I compared it to an unidentified clipping that had no date but had been in Quincy's file. All the subjects are of venerable age and there is a cannon hidden below a draped U.S. flag. This must have been a group of old soldiers at a reunion of some sort. Was it an earlier reunion of Company G? The flat-topped straw "boater" hats were popular circa the 1920s. I also wondered where it was taken. I asked my aunt if she recognized the site and she replied, "That's Grandpa's reunion at Montour Falls [NY], I think!" Montour Falls was near where he and Nellie lived in Elmira Heights in his later years and is a long way from Haverhill, MA. Some of the girls went to college in Elmira, New York. At least four of the gentlemen are wearing reunion ribbons and two appear to have G.A.R. badges, visible under the magnifying glass. It is probably a gathering of a local G.A.R. post. I made a copy of the last four remaining members of Company G from the reunion identified as being from September 1927. I held it above the undated picture and tried to match the faces in the assembled draped-cannon group. I immediately recognized Quincy. He seemed more robust looking than in the clippings dated 1927. I can only surmise that this photograph was taken several years earlier, probably in the early 1920s, and probably at a local G.A.R. post gathering.

And then there were just two!

1928

BOSTON HERALD, FRIDAY, SEPTEMBER 14,

CIVIL WAR TRIO WHO MEET TODAY

ft to right, William M. Dresser, 99, of Haverhill; George W. Heath, 89, o averhill; John Quincy Adams, 84, of Rowley, are the sole survivors of compan G, 35th Massachusetts Infantry.

ONLY SURVIVORS OF CO. G, 35TH MASS DINE TODAY

HAVERHILL. Sept. 13—The three surviving members of company G, 35th Massachusetts infantry, will hold their annual reunion and dinner tomorrow, the anniversary of the battle of South Mountain, at the home of George W. Heath, 28 Moore street. South Mountain was the first battle in which the company was engaged in the civil war. Three days later the men fought in the famous battle of Antietam, after which all of the company's 101 men, except eight, were either dead or wounded.

The veterans meeting tomorrow are Mr. Heath, who is past commander of Maj. How post, O. A. R. of Haverhill; Past Quartermaster William M. Dresser and John Quincy Adams of Rowley, who is a member of post 50, O. A. R. of Peabody. Mr. Dresser lost a leg at Antietam. The 35th regiment will hold its 62d reunion Monday at the home of Mrs. Ella P. Long at 103 Hemenway street, Boston.

ca. 1927: Using the same photograph from the previous year, the *Boston Herald* **has removed M. L. Stover, leaving only three to attend the 1928 reunion dinner on the anniversary of the Battle of South Mountain.**

VETERANS OF CO. G GATHER FOR REUNION

(Gazette Staff Photo)

William Dresser, age 89; M. L. Stover, age 89, George W. Heath, age 87 and John Q. Adams, age 83, of Rowley.

William M. Dresser, Civil war veteran, was host yesterday at his home, Buttonwoods avenue, to Martin L. Stover, George W. Heath and John Adams, at a reunion of the survivors of Co. G, 35th regiment of Massachusetts Volunteers, who dined with him at noon.

These four, members of Major How Post, 47, G. A. R., left this city Aug. 27, 1862, and Sept. 14, were in the battle of South Mountain. This date of the first battle in which they were engaged has been observed by them each year since.

Their friendship has been continu-ous since boyhood days. During a smoke talk replete with reminiscence the menu served was contrasted with the rations of 65 years ago. A feature of the day's observance was the posing for a group picture.

The combined age of these veterans according to their next birthdays is 352 years. Mr. Adams, youngest of the four and will be 84 Feb. 17; Mr. Heath, past commander of Major How Post, will be 88, Oct. 5. Martin L. Stover, will be 90, Oct. 22. Mr. Dresser will be 90 Feb. 12.

Mr. Adams, a former piano teacher, played yesterday for the singing of "Marching Through Georgia," "Battle Hymn of the Republic," and "My Country 'Tis of Thee," led by Mr. Stover, only survivor of the G. A. R. quartet of the city. Mr. Stover added entertainment by reciting an original monolog in patriotic vein.

Mr. Adams now makes his home in Rowley and motored here yesterday for this reunion. Next year's reunion is looked forward to when Mr. Heath is to be the host. Mr. Dresser was assisted in the entertainment of his comrades by his daughters. Miss Wilhelmina K. Dresser and Miss Henrietta R. Dresser. The rooms were decorated with garden flowers.

Present at the 1927 reunion were the last four members of Co. G: William Dresser, age eighty-nine; M. L. Stover, age eighty-nine; George W. Heath, age eighty-seven, and Quincy at age eighty-three. Quincy and George Heath are identifiable in the larger group of an earlier year. By the 1928 reunion only three will remain. Mr. M. L. Stover had passed away.

Quincy included these words in a letter sent between 1929 and 1930, to his granddaughter Ellen, the author's mother, during her first year at Elmira College in New York State. "Monday Morning, Dear Ellen . . . The grand Encampment of the G.A.R. meets in Portland Maine next September. I am planning to attend. There is only one left of my Co. besides myself and he is 91 and very feeble . . ." Quincy would pass away on July 8, 1931, at the age of eighty-seven and Nellie would follow in 1936, at the age of eighty.

A portion of Quincy's letter to the author's mother in 1929–30, about a year or so before his passing in 1931

PARADE OF THE GRAND ARMY OF THE REPUBLIC.
Washington, D.C. September 26th 1892.

The parade of the Grand Army of the Republic, Washington, D.C., September 26, 1892, was captured by this wonderful print. Quincy would have been forty-nine and very active in the G.A.R. Judging by the existing letters from his senior years, he was able to, and apparently did, travel as far as Antietam and Fredericksburg for veterans' gatherings and celebrations. It seems safe to suppose that Quincy would not have missed this parade. Artifact courtesy of the Kevin Umhey Collection

QUINCY'S LEGACY

As a lover of music, Quincy would have been pleased that in the same year of his passing, 1931, Congress proclaimed "The Star-Spangled Banner" the national anthem of the United States, and that he had participated in keeping those states united. Being a Haverhill native, I am also sure that he was proud of having been a part of the event that helped America on the way to fully understanding that the word "men," in "all men are created equal . . ." *really* means "all human beings."

I found hidden among a stack of photos, a letter written by Affix J. Chandler to his daughter-in-law, Sylvia Adams, upon Quincy's passing. It provided me with words for an epitaph for a man to whom I now feel a strong kinship even though he was gone before my time.

Last known formal photograph of Quincy

Thursday A.M.
July 18th 1931.

My very dear Mrs. Adams!–

Yours of July 8 received and cannot half tell you how sorry I am to hear the very sad news of Mr. Adams's death, it was a great surprise to me. He had lived to a great age and had lived a good life. People knew him respected him and had only good to say of him. I am so pleased he was with Herbert. He called here only a short time before he went on his visit to you and he seemed very happy told me about it and I was pleased for him. I thought he had failed quite a little since I had seen him but for a person eighty-seven years of age he was a wonder. I am glad I saw him and asked him to play for me, he granted my request and it made me very happy he played beautifully and with the same soul. He was a splendid Teacher. I shall never forget his kindness to me. [I] shall never forget either him or Ella . . . . . . much love to Herbert, to your dear children and your dear self and thanks for your kindness to me.

Yours very sincerely, Affix J. Chandler

Among the family's old pictures I discovered one that speaks volumes of his most enduring legacy, a large, loving family. It was taken near his home in the last years of his life. It includes his wife, Nellie, his only son, Herbert, and his four grand-daughters. These granddaughters would have thirteen children, including this author.

White-mustached patriarch John Quincy Adams can be seen just to the right of the center window, sans hat. His only son, Herbert, and Herbert's wife, Sylvia, the author's maternal grandparents, stand by the left window on either side of Ella, in dark dress with white collar, Quincy's wife. The author's own mother, Ellen, is the dark-haired young girl seated on the far left. Her youngest and only surviving sister, Barbara, the principal guardian of Quincy's memorabilia in our time, is the little blond in between Ellen and Jeanie, her oldest sister. Jeanie had become the guardian of the Hunkins collection, which has now been past to me. Alice is the little girl seventh from the left. The photo was taken about 1923 in front of the Old Sawyer House, home of the Town Improvement Society, in Merrimac, Massachusetts, just east of Haverhill.

Perhaps the last of Quincy's artifacts to be discovered, or rediscovered, was a wonderful old musket that my father had found in the attic of the old Alpine,

New York, home of Herbert and Sylvia Adams in the late 1940s. This was the house of my early memories and the home of that wonderful old bugle. Had Grandpa inherited it from Quincy? The old musket's stock had been painted red. My dad had painstakingly cleaned the gun, revealing its beautiful birds-eye maple stock. It was in firing condition and was accompanied by all the necessary shooting material. In the accompanying cache of accoutrements were: two full powder horns, two waterproof containers also filled with black powder, a number of leather wades and their punch, a bag of shot, and two full primer tins. The gun hung in the living room of our home until I inherited it upon my father's passing. Herbert was a draftsman with the American Bridge Company and though he was a gentleman farmer, I never heard that he was a sportsman or a shooter. The style and technology would have predated Quincy's senior years, but it could have been a relic of his youth. There is a high probability that this old smoothbore belonged to Quincy or perhaps his father, George Whitfield Adams, as Quincy may have lived with his son, Herbert, and daughter-in-law, Sylvia, for some time in his later years. Whatever its true story, it now hangs in my studio and will forever remind me of that part of my family's heritage.

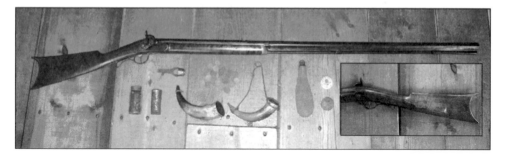

The Adamses' family gun with all its accoutrements

Today Quincy lies next to his wife in Woodlawn Cemetery, Elmira, New York. This is the community where he and Nellie had moved in his final years to be near his son, daughter-in-law, Sylvia, and his four granddaughters. They lie quite close to Mark Twain, in the town where Twain did most of his writing. Sadly, nearby are the graves of many thousands of his old Confederate adversaries. Elmira was the site of the most infamous prisoner-of-war camp in the North, perhaps second only to its Confederate counterpart in infamy, Andersonville Prison in Macon County, Georgia. Many more Union soldiers lie in the adjacent Woodlawn National Cemetery, all at peace now.

We located Quincy and Nellie's final resting place in Woodlawn Cemetery in Elmira, New York. Apparently I have inherited Quincy's eyes and mustache.

When I ponder Quincy's later life, one word comes to mind most often, and that word is "dignity." Aristotle is credited as saying: "Dignity does not consist in possessing honors, but in deserving them." Quincy bore his war with quiet dignity, survived it, and came home to live a good and honorable life as a teacher, father, and grandfather. Although he wouldn't live to know it, he would become a great-grandfather to thirteen great-grandchildren, good citizens all. Just for fun I started adding up all the great-great grandchildren and there are over a dozen and a half, some starting on the next generation. I recall the reverence shown by my grandmother and his four granddaughters to his memory, manifested by the care of his memorabilia; I am envious of not having known him in person. I have come to know Quincy only through photographs, artifacts, and especially his journal. Without these treasures his story could not have been reconstructed and shared with the future. I think of all the journals and artifacts of countless common soldiers who served their country and cause, all the while, enduring uncommon hardships. By most estimates there were over 700,000 soldier deaths and countless others who were maimed for life as a result of the Civil War. Soldiers whose families have lost the memory of all these common folks who performed uncommon deeds in the service of their country as best they knew; soldiers North and South who endured the countless miles of mud, toil, and boredom, occasionally punctuated by the extreme horror of battle. Most of the Billy Yank and Johnny Reb stories have now vanished. Hopefully this work will serve to encourage others to discover their own ancestors, before it is too late.

Eleven of Quincy's great-grandchildren are pictured here. Sadly, the twelfth, Lenora, had passed away at the age of three. These formed the troop of "want-to-be soldiers" at Alpine, New York, ca. 1952. The author is fourth from the right.

JOHN QUINCY ADAMS

Born, Feb. 17, 1844.
Married Eleanor Wight Hunkins,
Dec. 13, 1875

Died, July 8, 1931.
Buried, Elmira, New York,
July 11.

Whereas, another member of our Association has been called from this life to the life beyond,—a member who, as a veteran of the Civil War, was well-known, loved and respected by all who knew him, a member who was always present at our meetings, and

Whereas

"We shall meet, but we shall miss him,
There will be one vacant chair."

A motion passed by a family association of which Quincy was a member.

DEDICATION

Dedicated to Frederick Heimes Senior (1918-1945)

This book is dedicated to all the American service personnel who served their country in time of need, and in particular one **Frederick Heimes.** Fred was born on April 26, 1918 in Webster NY. After graduating from Cornell University; he married Quincy's granddaughter, Barbara Adams, on January 1, 1942. Fred joined the United States Army in August, 1943 and deployed to France with the 254th Infantry, 63rd Division in late November of 1944. Arriving in Marseilles in early December of that year, Fred and the 254th fought the wehrmacht in the "Colmar Pocket" in the Alsace region of France. This was one of the bitterest campaigns of the war in Europe. In March, 1945 the regiment began the attack on the "Siegfried Line", the "impenetrable" West Wall of Germany in temperatures of minus 20º Celsius. On March 17, 1945, while serving as acting Platoon Leader in this assault on the outskirts of Ensheim, Germany, Fred was killed during a heavy barrage of mortar and artillery from German positions. After five days they had broken through the fortifications that took the Germans seven years to construct. The 254th was awarded the Presidential Citation for this action. Fred had given his life for his country.

ACKNOWLEDGMENTS

The family of John Quincy Adams who so dutifully preserved his memory for these past years (an asterisk indicates a direct descendant of our John Quincy Adams):

Herbert* and Sylvia Adams

Barbara Coats*

Clem and Ellen* Angstrom

Peter Coats*

Virginia Barone*

Virginia Cutler*

John Barone*

Alice Train*

Frederick Heimes Jr.*

The family and friends, old and new, who helped in many different ways to bring Quincy's story out of the attics of time and make it possible to share it with future family and the public.

Encouragement and support:

My wife, life partner, and best friend, Catherine (Duffy) Angstrom

Michael L. Angstrom*

Adrienne (Angstrom) Silvia*

Alexandria Silvia*

Tommy Silvia*

John Kemnitzer

Technical support and advice—proofreading, ideas, and valuable suggestions:

Andrew D. Angstrom*

Richard Kirgan

Michael L. Angstrom*

Patricia Davis

Kevin Umhey

Heather Angstrom

Family members who graciously shared their Quincy artifacts and memorabilia:

John Barone*

Virginia Cutler*

Barbara Coats*

Peter Coats*

Frederick Heimes*

David Train*

Historic information and collections:

  Alan Coon

  Massachusetts Art Commission

  Kevin Umhey

  United States Army Heritage and Education Center, Carlisle, PA

  —MOLLUS-Mass. Civil War Photograph Collection

A special thanks:

  Bill Frueh, musician, 77th New York Volunteer Infantry

  Jay Ungar, Molly Mason and the Ashokan Center for the Arts, History, and Environmental Education

  Susan Greendyke Lachevre, Massachusetts Art Commission

  Marlea D. Leljedal, U.S. Army Heritage and Education Center, Carlisle, PA

  Jake Struhelka, staff, Fredericksburg National Battlefield

  Members of the 150th New York Volunteer Infantry

In memory of our precious daughter, Adrienne Anne (Angstrom) Silvia

SELECTED BIBLIOGRAPHY

Albert, Alphaeus H. *Record of American Uniform and Historical Buttons* (Boyertown, PA: Boyertown Publishing Co., 1977).

Bailey, Ronald H. *The Bloodiest Day: The Battle of Antietam* (New York: Time-Life Books, Inc., 1984).

Bowman, John, general editor. *Chronicles of the Civil War* (North Dighton, MA: World Publications, 2005).

Campbell, J. Duncan and Edgar M. Howell. *American Military Insignia 1800–1851* originally published by the Smithsonian Institute, as United States National Museum Bulletin number 235, 1963. Reprinted by (Confederate States Press: Baton Rouge, LA).

Coggins, Jack. *Arms and Equipment of the Civil War* (Wilmington, NC: Broadfoot Publishing Co., 1962).

Davis, William C. *The Battlefields of the Civil War* (London: Salamander Books Ltd.). 1991

Davis, William C. *The Fighting Men of the Civil War* (New York: Smithmark Publishers Inc.). 1991

Foster, Joseph. *The Dictionary of Heraldry: Feudal Coats of Arms and Pedigrees* (New York: Bracken Books, Arch Cape Press, 1989).

Gardner, Alexander. *Gardner's Photographic Sketchbook of the Civil War* (New York: Dover Publishing Inc., 1959).

Garrison, Webb. *Civil War Curiosities, Strange Stories, Oddities, Events, and Coincidences* (Nashville: Rutledge Hill Press, 1994).

Hendricks, Howard. *The City of Kingston, Birth place of New York State* (Kingston, NY: Kingston Board of Trade, 1902).

Johnson, Swafford. *Great Battles of the Civil War* (New York: Exeter Books, 1st/Bison Books, 1984).

Jordan, Robert Paul. *The Civil War* (National Geographic Society, 1969, Washington, D.C.).

Katcher, Phillip. *The Civil War Day by Day* (New York: Chartwell Books Inc., 2007).

Kautz, August V. *The 1865 Customs of Service for Non-commissioned Officers and Soldiers, (U.S) Handbook* (Mechanicsburg, PA: Stackpole Books, 2001).

Kerksis, Sydney C. *Plates and Buckles of the American Military 1795–1874* (Kennesaw, Georgia: Kennesaw Mountain Press, 1974, ed. 1991).

Lord, Francis A. *Civil War Collector's Encyclopedia, Vol. I & II* (Edison, NJ: Blue & Gray Press, 1995).

Lossing, J. Benson. *Mathew Brady's Illustrated History of the Civil War with His War Photographs and Paintings by Military Artists* (New York: Grammercy, 1994).

McManus, Stephen, Donald Thompson, and Thomas Churchill. *The Civil War Research Guide* (Mechanicsburg, PA: Stackpole Books, 2003).

Miller, William Lee. *Arguing about Slavery: John Quincy Adams and the Great Battle in the United States Congress* (New York: Vintage Books, 1995).

Noble, Trinka Hakes, illustrated by Robert Papp. *The Last Brother: A Civil War Tale* (Chelsea, MI: Sleeping Bear Press, 2006).

Smith, Carl and Michael Spilling, ed. *Fredericksburg 1862 (Osprey Trade Edition)* (Wellingborough, UK: Osprey Publishing Ltd., 1999).

Stevens, Norman S. *Antietam 1862: The Civil War's Bloodiest Day* (Oxford, UK: Osprey Publishing Ltd., 1994).

Styple, William B. *The Little Bugler* (Kearny, NJ: Belle Grove Publishing Co., 1998).

Thomas, Dean S. *Cannons: An Introduction to Civil War Artillery, 14th Ed.* (Gettysburg, PA: Thomas Publications, 1985).

United States Army Massachusetts Infantry Regiment, *History of the Thirty-Fifth Regiment Massachusetts Volunteers, 1862–1865. With a Roster* (Boston: Mills, Knight & Co.,1884), reprinted by **Kessinger Publishing, 2012 ISBN 0548967377, 2012**

U.S. War Department, *The 1863 U.S. Infantry Tactics* (Mechanicsburg, PA: Stackpole Books, 2002).

Ward, Geoffrey C., with Ric Burns and Ken Burns. *The Civil War: An Illustrated History* (New York: Alfred A. Knopf, 1990).

Picture Credits

All photographs, charts and maps are the property of the author except for those identified with a courtesy note in the caption.

Sources of images other than those of the author:

- Library of Congress
- United States National Archives
- U.S. Army Heritage and Education Center, the MOLLUS-MASS Civil War
- Commonwealth of Massachusetts Art Commission
- The Commonwealth of Massachusetts